ALICE CAMILLE

W9-AGP-418

2009

A BOOK OF GRACE-FILLED DAYS

LOYOLA PRESS.
A JESUIT MINISTRY
CHICAGO

LOYOLA PRESS.

A JESUIT MINISTRY

3441 N. ASHLAND AVENUE
CHICAGO, ILLINOIS 60657
(800) 621-1008
WWW.LOYOLAPRESS.ORG

Cover and interior design by Kathy Kikkert

Library of Congress Cataloging-in-Publication Data

Camille, Alice L.
  2009 : a book of grace-filled days / Alice Camille.
     p. cm.
  ISBN-13: 978-0-8294-2524-6
  ISBN-10: 0-8294-2524-1
  1. Devotional calendars—Catholic Church. 2. Catholic Church—Prayers and devotions. 3. Bible—Meditations. 4. Catholic Church. Lectionary for Mass (U.S.). Year A. I. Title. II. Title: Two thousand nine. III. Title: Book of grace-filled days.
  BX2170.C56C36 2008
  242'.2--dc22

                                                          2008008079

 Printed in the United States of America
 08 09 10 11 12 13 Bang 10 9 8 7 6 5 4 3 2 1

INTRODUCTION

Every book is a world.

As a lover of books, I've been entering other worlds religiously—yes, religiously—since I was a kid. Before there were movies, television, and the Internet, books supplied the "great escape" for which the human spirit is often secretly yearning. It's not that the world at large isn't marvelous in many respects. But each of us contains multitudes, as Walt Whitman wrote in his epic poem, *Song of Myself.* Sometimes living this one little life just doesn't give us the room to express all that's available inside.

The expansiveness that we sense within us is no accident. It's the best definition I can come up with for the spiritual life. Jesus once described the realm of God as a mansion with many rooms. This is a great image for the spiritual quest as well. Our faith encompasses many riches, like so many rooms to explore and savor. First of all, there's Story, chief among which is the story of salvation unfolding in the Bible.

And there's a room for the Saints, whose past example and continuing presence provide us with comforting and challenging companionship. We've also got a place for Prayer, Public Worship, Church History, and Wise Teaching. We could wander through these rooms for a lifetime and never exhaust their potential for illumination and delight.

This little book provides a path for wandering through those rooms. It's not a perfect, one-size-fits-all trail, as I'll be first to admit. Some of us are more naturally inclined to lead with our hearts and others with our heads. Some view the spiritual quest as one of seeking wisdom, knowledge, and understanding—a *learning* process. Others equate learning with homework, and would rather *feel* than think their way through to a genuine religious experience. Some of us are frankly in it for the sake of a good story, or a single word or image that will spark us into renewed life. Me personally, I like surprises, and I'm always grateful to anyone who can make me laugh. Even and especially in the realm of religion!

But most of all, when wandering through soul territory, what I'm looking for is a fire-breathing, Pentecostal rousing of the person God created me to be. That's the person stamped with the likeness of God. I don't know that woman as well as I might want. I sense her around the corner sometimes.

When the breath of the Spirit flutters through me in rare moments, I feel my true name being spoken and what might be called my "holy self" rising. So let me say without embarrassment that I want to be holy: what other reason is there to live a Christian life? If you're reading this book, chances are you want to be a holy person too.

Holiness doesn't require a halo, folded hands, or an otherworldly preoccupation. But it does involve the action of grace. Grace is a gift from God that we can't earn but that God earnestly desires to shower down on anyone willing to stand still long enough to get doused. So consider this book an opportunity to stand still together for a few minutes every day this year, to allow the grace of each hour to rain down on us. Please don't beat yourself up if you miss a day. This isn't spinach; there's no punitive angle here. Enter the world of this book when you can, for the sake of the adventure into grace. Risk everything you have and everything you are on God's promises. See what happens. The results could be glorious.

Watch, therefore; you do not know when the lord of the house is coming, whether in the evening, or at midnight, or at cockcrow, or in the morning.

—Mark 13:35

Time dribbles through our fingers while we wait. Life falls into a holding pattern in checkout lines, on subway platforms, in airports, or in traffic jams. We await payday, test results, or the first glimpse of the one face that matters. We turn toward what's coming with excitement, dread— and, sometimes, joyful hope. And in Advent, we do one thing more: we wait *watchfully*. God will break into time like a thief. What will the holy one find locked in our hearts?

Isaiah 63:16b–17, 19b; 64:2–7
Psalm 80
1 Corinthians 1:3–9
Mark 13:33–37

⇒ 1 ⇐

DECEMBER 1

Come, let us climb the LORD's mountain,
to the house of the God of Jacob,
That he may instruct us in his ways,
and we may walk in his paths.

—ISAIAH 2:3

After midnight, our small group began the ascent of a mountain on the Sinai Peninsula believed to be the one Moses climbed to meet God. Thirty-three hundred years ago, Moses did it without a guide, a warm coat, or a flashlight. As we climbed, the wind bit hard; I stopped looking over the sheer drop. We made the crest at dawn. Would God be manifest, after our hours of striving? An Arab man sat on top of the mountain, crouched over a fire. "Some tea?" he asked. In English. God was here!

Isaiah 2:1–5
Psalm 122
Matthew 8:5–11

Turning to the disciples in private {Jesus} said, "Blessed are the eyes that see what you see."

—LUKE 10:23

Life is good! From where you are, you can probably see something that would astound prophets and kings of old. Are electric lights gleaming above you? Is food being kept at a carefully calibrated temperature in your fridge? Does a loved one's face smile at you from a photograph? Still, the greatest blessings are seen only through the eyes of faith: the presence of Jesus in word and sacrament, in suffering and healing, in death and fullness of life.

Isaiah 11:1–10
Psalm 72
Luke 10:21–24

Even when I walk through a dark valley,
I fear no harm for you are at my side;
your rod and staff give me courage.

—PSALM 23:4

The dark valley haunts us all our lives. Francis Xavier longed to bring the gospel to China, but after evangelizing India and Malaysia, he died within sight of his heart's desire. Our mortality may catch up with us before we pay off the house, raise the kids, or fulfill our dreams. The very definition of our humanity may be this: life is over before we're finished. "Finished" doesn't matter; it's "faithful" that we're after. Fidelity is the greatest legacy we can leave behind.

Isaiah 25:6–10a
Psalm 23
Matthew 15:29–37

DECEMBER 4

• ST. JOHN OF DAMASCUS, PRIEST AND DOCTOR OF THE CHURCH •

The LORD is God and has given us light.
—PSALM 118:27

In the eighth century, iconoclasts destroyed sacred images, believing that the Eucharist alone should represent the divine on earth. John of Damascus argued that images help connect us to the invisible realities of heaven. Have you ever encountered religious art and been captured by the truth you discovered there? Artists participate in the divine activity of creation. Surely God still says, through the artist: "Let there be light."

Isaiah 26:1–6
Psalm 118
Matthew 7:21, 24–27

DECEMBER 5

One thing I ask of the LORD;
this I seek:
To dwell in the LORD's house
all the days of my life,
To gaze on the LORD's beauty,
to visit his temple.

—PSALM 27:4

Looking for God? Look for beauty. Dante understood
this when he wrote *The Divine Comedy* and described the
"Beatific Vision" of God. He borrowed this idea from
the psalmist, but also from Exodus. There, in chapter 33,
Moses begs to see the God he faithfully serves. God gently
refuses—mortal life cannot withstand the sight—but offers
instead to reveal "all my beauty." When we stand in awe of
loveliness, we get a glimpse of what Moses saw.

Isaiah 29:17–24
Psalm 27
Matthew 9:27–31

DECEMBER 6

• ST. NICHOLAS, BISHOP •

Cure the sick, raise the dead, cleanse lepers, drive out demons. Without
cost you have received; without cost you are to give.

—MATTHEW 10:8

Cure the sick? Who wouldn't unleash such power if
they could? I sat with my friend in the oncology unit as
he awaited radiation treatment. Surveying a roomful of
courageous patients, I fiercely longed for miracles
to sweep down and anoint every head. But all I was able
to give my friend was a steady gaze into his suffering and
hopeful eyes.

Isaiah 30:19–21, 23–26
Psalm 147
Matthew 9:35–10:1, 5a, 6–8

But according to his promise we await new heavens and a new earth in which righteousness dwells.

—2 PETER 3:13

"New" is what we need. The old world is frayed and broken in a lot of places. We mend it from time to time with diplomacy and charity, or prop it up with environmental measures, military threats, and economic incentives. But human history remains the worse for wear. Yet we can't just throw up our hands and abandon the place. It's all we've got! So we continue to work for justice and peace, all the while praying for that kingdom to come.

Isaiah 40:1–5, 9–11
Psalm 85
2 Peter 3:8–14
Mark 1:1–8

Monday
DECEMBER 8

• THE IMMACULATE CONCEPTION OF THE BLESSED VIRGIN MARY •

Then the angel said to her, "Do not be afraid, Mary, for you have found favor with God."

—LUKE 1:30

Mary's heart was remarkable. Even God fell in love with her! And so have billions of folks since. A Marian sanctuary in Altötting, Bavaria, preserves in silver urns the actual hearts of kings and princes who swore special allegiance to Mary. Probably no one will ever place my heart in a shrine. But there are other ways to surrender our hearts like Mary did.

Genesis 3:9–15, 20
Psalm 98
Ephesians 1:3–6, 11–12
Luke 1:26–38

⇒ 9 ⇐

Tell God's glory among the nations;
among all peoples, God's marvelous deeds.

—PSALM 96:3

Juan Diego was nobody, really. Just a Mexican Indian of a defeated people who had barely survived the bloody European conquest of 1521. Their homes had been burned, their men killed, their women raped, and their temples destroyed. Juan Diego and his people did not have much to live for. Yet to them and in their likeness, the Virgin appeared and promised her protection. Even when you're nobody, heaven is watching.

Isaiah 40:1–11
Psalm 96
Matthew 18:12–14

DECEMBER 10

Come to me, all you who labor and are burdened, and I will give you rest.

—MATTHEW 11:28

I know a man who was rescued by these simple words. He was a stockbroker, successful in terms of money, personal attraction, and career potential. He was also an alcoholic at the mercy, night and day, of his "gorgeous thirst."

One Advent night, he slumped into the back pew of a church while Mass was going on. He heard Jesus promise to take his burden away. How he longed for such rest! He quit drinking. Today he's proclaiming this hope to others as a priest.

Isaiah 40:25–31
Psalm 103
Matthew 11:28–30

DECEMBER 11

• ST. DAMASUS I, POPE •

From the days of John the Baptist until now, the kingdom of heaven
suffers violence, and the violent are taking it by force.

—MATTHEW 11:12

Can heaven be taken by force? Or can violence ever serve
God's purposes? Scriptures can be gathered to support one
side of this argument and the other. Wars have been fought
in the name of religion, both armies blessed as they go
into battle. Conversions have been gained at the point of a
sword. Many simply are frightened into obedience by the
pains of hell. Yet how can the realm of a God who is love
ever be entered except through love's own free surrender?

Isaiah 41:13–20
Psalm 145
Matthew 11:11–15

DECEMBER 12

• OUR LADY OF GUADALUPE •

Blessed are you who believed that what was spoken to you by the Lord would be fulfilled.

—LUKE 1:45

Visions and angels and saints, oh my! Private revelations are by definition not for everyone, and the church teaches that belief in them is not mandatory. Yet many find the apparitions of Mary both instructive and encouraging to their faith. As the Virgin of Guadalupe, Mary said, "I want to be your mother. I want to right the wrongs." Sure sounds like heaven talking, don't you think?

Zechariah 2:14–17 or Revelation 11:19a; 12:1–6a, 10ab
Psalm 45
Luke 1:26–38 or 1:39–47

How awesome are you, ELIJAH!
Whose glory is equal to yours? . . .
You were taken aloft in a whirlwind,
in a chariot with fiery horses.

—SIRACH 48:4, 9

I always expected God to appear in a glorious display,
as when the fiery chariot snatches Elijah into heaven. I
was hoping for the God of Cecil B. DeMille. Sometimes,
however, God is more like George Burns.

Sirach 48:1–4, 9–11
Psalm 80
Matthew 17:9a, 10–13

DECEMBER 14

• THIRD SUNDAY OF ADVENT •

When the Jews from Jerusalem sent priests and Levites [to {John}] to ask him, "Who are you?" he admitted and did not deny it, but admitted, "I am not the Messiah."

—JOHN 1:19–20

"Finding yourself" is a highly overrated imperative. It doesn't matter so much that we know precisely who we are—especially since a human being is always growing and changing anyway. But it sure helps to know who we're *not*. We're not God, for one. We're not even close, not on our best days. John's final answer regarding his identity is instructive: he's a voice in an empty place announcing God's arrival. We should all be so clear about our reason for being!

Isaiah 61:1–2a, 10–11
Luke 1:46–50, 53–54
1 Thessalonians 5:16–24
John 1:6–8, 19–28

The utterance of Balaam, son of Beor,
the utterance of the man whose eye is true. . . .
I see him, though not now;
I behold him, though not near:
A star shall advance from Jacob,
and a staff shall rise from Israel.
—NUMBERS 24:15, 17

The whole passage, chapters 22–24, is worth a read. The story of Balaam and his ass is the only anecdote of a talking animal outside of Eden—and the donkey isn't the only ass in the tale. Balaam becomes a true prophet the hard way, by being brought to his knees by God. We all learn humility the hard way, it seems, but it's the only way to become a person "whose eye is true."

Numbers 24:2–7, 15–17a
Psalm 25
Matthew 21:23–27

DECEMBER 16

*They shall do no wrong
and speak no lies;
Nor shall there be found in their mouths
a deceitful tongue.*
—ZEPHANIAH 3:13

Truth is an attribute of God. It's a big deal in both the Old and the New Testament: giving false testimony earns a "You shall not" among the Ten Commandments. Jesus calls himself "the truth." But we live in an age of spin, image management, retouched photography, and cosmetic surgery. Truth, frankly, is not our deal. Pilate's ancient lament might be raised today: What is truth? How do we become people of truth in an age dependent on illusions?

Zephaniah 3:1–2, 9–13
Psalm 34
Matthew 21:28–32

Wednesday
DECEMBER 17

The scepter shall never depart from Judah.
—GENESIS 49:10

The lineage of Jesus runs through Judah. During the week before Christmas, the church has traditionally honored the human and divine origins of Jesus in the "O Antiphons." We know them as the familiar verses of "O Come, O Come, Emmanuel." The first antiphon, O Wisdom, reminds us that all of creation was ordered by God's own wisdom— the only "intelligent design" we'll ever need. God's wisdom is shared with us as one of the seven gifts of the Holy Spirit. Pray for wisdom. Seek it. Share it.

Genesis 49:2, 8–10
Psalm 72
Matthew 1:1–17

She will bear a son and you are to name him Jesus, because he will save his people from their sins.

—MATTHEW 1:21

Today's antiphon is a Hebrew name: O Adonai. It's a respectful title usually translated "Lord" or "Master." Although God gave the divine name to Moses as "I AM WHO AM," folks were reluctant to abuse the privilege of using it. In John's Gospel, Jesus insists on saying "I AM" a lot—bringing the accusation of blasphemy. St. Paul proclaimed boldly, "Jesus is Lord"—take it or leave it. Most of the time, we leave it. What would happen if we took it seriously?

Jeremiah 23:5–8
Psalm 72
Matthew 1:18–25

An angel of the LORD appeared to the woman and said to her, "Though you are barren and have had no children, yet you will conceive and bear a son."

—JUDGES 13:3

The situation is hopeless, yet God promises the impossible. Is it Mary of Nazareth who receives this news? This time, actually, it's the mother of Samson—but it could just as well have been Sarah, Hannah, the Shunammite woman, or Elizabeth. Or maybe even you or someone you know. God's in the "impossible" business. "O Root of Jesse" is the name we celebrate today, because new life keeps coming from that surprising source.

Judges 13:2–7, 24–25a
Psalm 71
Luke 1:5–25

Therefore the Lord himself will give you this sign: the virgin shall be
with child, and bear a son, and shall name him Immanuel.

—ISAIAH 7:14

I'm not always good at reading the signs. The sky may be threatening, but I leave the umbrella behind. My wallet is empty, but I count on finding an ATM wherever I am. I eat past the moment I am full. I'm tempted by easy money, even though I know there's no such thing. O Key of David, unlock my foolish heart and help me take the signs of your truth more seriously!

Isaiah 7:10–14
Psalm 24
Luke 1:26–38

[. . . according to the revelation of the mystery kept secret for long ages but now manifested through the prophetic writings . . .]

—ROMANS 16:25–26

The meaning of the events of our lives often dawns slowly. What started out as a simple childhood hobby leads to a lifelong passion. A chance meeting becomes a marriage. A tiny spiritual tap on the shoulder awakens a religious vocation. O Radiant Dawn, you arrive on our doorstep while we are still half-asleep. Open our eyes to the great blessing you always have in store for us.

2 Samuel 7:1–5, 8b–12, 14a, 16
Psalm 89
Romans 16:25–27
Luke 1:26–38

{The LORD} raises the needy from the dust;
from the ash heap he lifts up the poor,
To seat them with nobles
and make a glorious throne their heritage.

—1 SAMUEL 2:8

In old-world societies, "rich" and "poor" were immutable
social classes. Those born rich tended to remain in such
circles, and those born poor would never amount to much.
Part of the American Dream is the idea that one can arise
from humble beginnings to achieve greatness. Social class
is dismissed as merely an illusion or a temporary condition.
O King of Nations, help us see that the last will be first,
and the first are destined to be last.

1 Samuel 1:24–28
1 Samuel 2:1, 4–8
Luke 1:46–56

All who heard these things took them to heart, saying, "What, then, will this child be?" For surely the hand of the Lord was with him.

—LUKE 1:66

John, aka the Baptist, seemed destined for greatness. Not much was expected of another John, however—a Polish fellow from Kanty. Ousted from his university professorship under false accusations, he wound up a parish priest in Bohemia. But he didn't protest his treatment: "Fight all error," he said, "but do it with good humor, patience, kindness, and love. Harshness will damage your own soul and spoil the best cause." O Emmanuel, I know well that the harshness I show toward others hurts me most of all.

Malachi 3:1–4, 23–24
Psalm 25
Luke 1:57–66

And you, child, will be called prophet of the Most High,
for you will go before the Lord to prepare his ways,
to give his people knowledge of salvation
through the forgiveness of their sins.

—LUKE 1:76–77

Boil Christianity down to its essence, and you end up with
one word: *forgiveness.* It's no one's favorite word, because
forgiving is one of the toughest things we'll do in this life.
It's an activity that presupposes a grievance, and the last
thing an injured person wants to do is let go of a just cause
for outrage. Eye-for-an-eye justice is the way of the world.
But it's not God's way. Not if Jesus is your Lord.

2 Samuel 7:1–5, 8b–12, 14a, 16
Psalm 89
Luke 1:67–79

And the Word became flesh
and made his dwelling among us,
and we saw his glory,
the glory as of the Father's only Son,
full of grace and truth.

—JOHN 1:14

Love is a word made flesh. There's no point in saying it
unless you're going to back it up with substance, with body
and blood, sweat and tears. That's how parents show love
to their children, lovers to their beloved, friends to their
comrades, and soldiers to their country. That's how saints
demonstrate their love for the God they follow, all the way
to martyrdom. So too the Word of God makes his fragile
way into the world, risking all for love's sake.

Vigil:
Isaiah 62:1–5
Psalm 89
Acts 13:16–17, 22–25
Matthew 1:1–25 or 1:18–25
Midnight:
Isaiah 9:1–6
Psalm 96
Titus 2:11–14
Luke 2:1–14
Dawn:
Isaiah 62:11–12
Psalm 97
Titus 3:4–7
Luke 2:15–20
Day:
Isaiah 52:7–10
Psalm 98
Hebrews 1:1–6
John 1:1–18 or 1:1–5, 9–14

The witnesses laid down their cloaks at the feet of a young man named Saul. As they were stoning Stephen, he called out, "Lord Jesus, receive my spirit."

—ACTS 7:58–59

Here is a strange and sudden turning point: the church grieves its first martyr in the hour it introduces its most celebrated missionary. The death of Stephen comes about at the feet of Saul. Saul is hardly an innocent bystander as he collects the coats. He's a ferocious hater of the new religion and its adherents. He regards God's law as immutable and wants to see lawbreakers punished. He must have heard Stephen's confident cries for God's mercy with incredulity.

Acts 6:8–10; 7:54–59
Psalm 31
Matthew 10:17–22

What was from the beginning,
what we have heard,
what we have seen with our eyes,
what we looked upon
and touched with our hands
concerns the Word of life.

—1 JOHN 1:1

The evangelists gave their testimony. They stood up in the court of human experience and witnessed to what they themselves had heard, seen, touched, and understood. We continue to benefit from their words, but it isn't enough to memorize and recite what they said. We have to find the courage to testify to what *we* have come to know through our own experiences. What do we really believe?

1 John 1:1–4
Psalm 97
John 20:1a, 2–8

Put on then, as God's chosen ones, holy and beloved, heartfelt compassion, kindness, humility, gentleness, and patience, bearing with one another and forgiving one another, if one has a grievance against another; as the Lord has forgiven you, so must you also do. And over all these put on love, that is, the bond of perfection.

—COLOSSIANS 3:12–14

I can't think of better words with which to advise a family on how to *be* a family. Without humility and gentleness as a foundation, relationships soon collapse under conflict. Without constantly renewed forgiveness (forget the easy math of seventy times seven!), intimacy is impossible. Without love, blood ties devolve into chains. Holy families are, first and foremost, havens of kindness.

Sirach 3:2–6, 12–14 or Genesis 15:1–6; 21:1–3
Psalm 128
Colossians 3:12–21 or 3:12–17 or Hebrews 11:8, 11–12, 17–19
Luke 2:22–40 or 2:22, 39–40

DECEMBER 29

• ST. THOMAS BECKET, BISHOP AND MARTYR •

Now, Master, you may let your servant go
in peace, according to your word.
—LUKE 2:29

The old year is on the wane. Time is among God's most
faithful servants, but sooner or later, even time pours itself
out into eternity like a humble tributary into the great
ocean. This past year gave each of us many opportunities
to practice the fruits of the Holy Spirit: love, joy, peace,
patience, kindness, generosity, faithfulness, gentleness,
and self-control. We embraced some, botched others. In
the spirit of reconciliation, let this past year go in peace.
Renew your resolve for the year ahead.

1 John 2:3–11
Psalm 96
Luke 2:22–35

*There was also a prophetess, Anna. . . . She was advanced in years,
having lived seven years with her husband after her marriage, and then
as a widow until she was eighty-four. She never left the temple, but
worshiped night and day with fasting and prayer.*

—LUKE 2:36–37

I know this woman. I think we all do. She gives every spare
moment to the church, every last dime to the needy. She
comes to every meeting and marches in every protest.
Every good cause is her cause. She knows everybody and
remembers the past with wisdom. She's old and her face is
weathered, but she has the high spirits of a teenager and
the optimism of a child. If you catch her praying in a dark
church, she glows.

1 John 2:12–17
Psalm 96
Luke 2:36–40

Wednesday

DECEMBER 31

• ST. SYLVESTER I, POPE •

Children, it is the last hour; and just as you heard that the antichrist was coming, so now many antichrists have appeared. . . . But you have the anointing that comes from the holy one, and you all have knowledge.

—1 JOHN 2:18, 20

Do you believe the end is near? I do. It doesn't take a prophet to know that in every moment, every cell in our bodies is moving toward its expiration date. Antichrists— those who move in a spirit contrary to the will of Christ— are much in evidence. Is our proximity to death and the reality of evil reason to fear? Not if we surrender our lives to the holy one, early and often.

1 John 2:18–21
Psalm 96
John 1:1–18

And Mary kept all these things, reflecting on them in her heart.
—LUKE 2:19

Want to start the New Year with a song in your heart?
Try one by John Lennon: "All we are saying is give
peace a chance." Lyrics about peace abound, but nations
rarely choose to hum a few bars. Pope John Paul II once
preached, "War should belong to the tragic past, to history:
it should find no place on humanity's agenda for the
future." To take war off the agenda, we first have to purge
our own hearts of fear and judgment.

Numbers 6:22–27
Psalm 67
Galatians 4:4–7
Luke 2:16–21

Friday

JANUARY 2

• ST. BASIL THE GREAT AND ST. GREGORY NAZIANZEN, BISHOPS AND
DOCTORS OF THE CHURCH •

So they said to {John the Baptist}, "Who are you, so we can give an
answer to those who sent us? What do you have to say for yourself?"
—JOHN 1:22

Pick a friend, any friend. Now imagine that you two
will persevere in the faith, become bright lights of holy
example to your generation, and share a feast day together
on the church calendar. This may stretch your religious
imagination, but it's just what happened to Saints Basil and
Gregory back in the fourth century. Consider it a (slightly
late) New Year's resolution and get your friend on board.
You can even have tee shirts made: "Saints in Progress."

1 John 2:22–28
Psalm 98
John 1:19–28

⇒ 35 ⇐

See what love the Father has bestowed on us that we may be called the children of God. Yet so we are.

—1 JOHN 3:1

Undeniably, names have power. And some are more powerful than others. That's why Norma Jean Baker became Marilyn Monroe, and Archibald Alexander Leach is known as Cary Grant. Even folks in the Bible knew better than to turn down an appellation upgrade. So Abram morphed into Abraham, Jacob into Israel, and Simon into Peter. Although many of us hang on to our original names, we share a designation more significant still: children of God. It's a name with a view and plenty of growing room.

1 John 2:29–3:6
Psalm 98
John 1:29–34

"Go and search diligently for the child. When you have found him, bring me word, that I too may go and do him homage."

—MATTHEW 2:8

King Herod wanted a diligent search for the child of prophecy—though not with homage in mind. He was full of fear, greed, and cruelty. So how come I, who really do mean to honor Jesus, search for him with far less zeal? My heart is likewise crowded with motivations: worship and self-interest, good intentions coupled with laziness. Christ is incarnate everywhere I look, in family and in strangers—especially in the eyes of those in need. No search is required. Only sincerity.

Isaiah 60:1–6
Psalm 72
Ephesians 3:2–3a, 5–6
Matthew 2:1–12

You belong to God, children, and you have conquered them, for the one who is in you is greater than the one who is in the world.

—1 JOHN 4:4

The word *bohemian* describes a wandering lifestyle. And it applies to John Neumann, who was born in Bohemia in 1811. When he dropped dead at fifty on the streets of Philadelphia, USA, he was the hardworking bishop of that diocese. He founded nearly 100 schools and 50 churches, and once walked twenty-five miles to confirm a sick child. John made "bohemian" look good on a bishop. Maybe it's the lifestyle for everyone convinced that the Spirit in us is greater than any obstacle.

1 John 3:22—4:6
Psalm 2
Matthew 4:12–17, 23–25

Beloved, let us love one another, because love is of God; everyone who loves is begotten by God and knows God.

—1 JOHN 4:7

Laborers, doorkeepers, and barbers—who looks for saints among their number? André Bessette, the Miracle Worker of Montreal, held all of these positions. Always in poor health, this lay brother was ill-suited to the priesthood. Yet his remarkable gift for healing the sick matched his deep humility in being "only a tool in the hands of Providence." However unassuming our role, our love may be the miracle someone is waiting for.

1 John 4:7–10
Psalm 72
Mark 6:34–44

JANUARY 7

• ST. RAYMOND OF PEÑAFORT, PRIEST •

But at once {Jesus} spoke with them, "Take courage, it is I, do not be afraid!" He got into the boat with them and the wind died down.

—MARK 6:50–51

If I've learned one lesson from reading the gospel, it's this: if Jesus isn't in your boat, don't even think of launching. You won't catch any fish and the storm will grow fierce. Without Jesus, you're wasting your time and endangering your life. And this is true, of course, even outside the pages of the Bible.

1 John 4:11–18
Psalm 72
Mark 6:45–52

JANUARY 8

{Jesus} said to them, "Today this scripture passage is fulfilled in your hearing."

—LUKE 4:21

How often have I sat in church stunned by a phrase proclaimed in the readings that had my name all over it? A familiar story heard since childhood suddenly becomes a branding iron marking me as God's own. So I scribble down the words, post them on my refrigerator, desk, or bathroom mirror, and study them till they're imprinted on my heart. Gradually the paper curls and fades and falls away. It doesn't matter. The words now live inside me.

1 John 4:19–5:4
Psalm 72
Luke 4:14–22a

Jesus stretched out his hand, touched {the leper}, and said, "I do will it. Be made clean."

—LUKE 5:13

It's true. Jesus wants us to be healed and whole; not just wants it, but *wills* it. And a little will in the New Testament goes a long way. Just think of what happened to Mary of Nazareth when she surrendered her will to God's, or when Jesus did the same in the Garden of Gethsemane. God's will is done—on earth as it is in heaven. All we have to do is agree to collaborate.

1 John 5:5–13
Psalm 147
Luke 5:12–16

Children, be on your guard against idols.
—1 JOHN 5:21

As a kid, I thought idol worship was silly. Shoot, who would be so dumb as to believe a *thing* could be God? Then I got older and started stockpiling my own idols. It's easy, so long as you rename them something innocent-sounding. For example, take the love of money and call it "financial security." And let's call injustice "pragmatism," and neglecting the world's poor "taking care of my own responsibilities first." Before you know it, we've got shrines in every corner.

1 John 5:14–21
Psalm 149
John 3:22–30

JANUARY 11

• THE BAPTISM OF THE LORD •

On coming up out of the water {Jesus} saw the heavens being torn open
and the Spirit, like a dove, descending upon him.

—MARK 1:10

A beautiful blown-glass bowl was passed among us.
Each person was invited to dip a hand into the water it
contained. Some automatically blessed themselves. Others
considered its cool, clear properties. As the bowl made its
journey, our teacher reflected on what water is: the source
of life, the greatest component of our bodies, vital for
crops, the answer to thirst, refreshing and cleansing,
a tranquil lake, an ocean of discovery, a fearsome power
that destroys and restores. We grew to respect what was in
that bowl.

Isaiah 42:1–4, 6–7 or 55:1–11
Psalm 29
Acts 10:34–38 or 1 John 5:1–9
Mark 1:7–11

JANUARY 12

Jesus said to them, "Come after me, and I will make you fishers of men."
Then they left their nets and followed him.

—MARK 1:17–18

It worries me, this scene at the edge of the sea. Fishermen
leaving their nets? Those ropes are their livelihood! Each
knot ties them to the world of consumable goods, food for
their families, a roof over their heads. Their nets are like
my computer, my credit cards, my checkbook. Jesus asks
these good folks to walk away from an occupation that is
secure and makes sense. He invites them to consider
a new catch, for which nets are useless. The implications
are staggering.

Hebrews 1:1–6
Psalm 97
Mark 1:14–20

*In their synagogue was a man with an unclean spirit; he cried out,
"What have you to do with us, Jesus of Nazareth? Have you come to
destroy us?"*

—MARK 1:23–24

Living with a bad spirit is an all-too-common experience. It
could be unquenchable rage, chronic depression, a hunger
for outside approval, or simple envy. This destructive
interior companion may become the dark love of our
lives. Hilary of Poitiers knew something about unholy
attachments. In one of his hymns he wrote: "Satan once
loved me ardently in the death {of sin}; let him behold me
reigning with Thee throughout the ages." The bad spirit is
a freeloader. Jesus has the power to evict.

Hebrews 2:5–12
Psalm 8
Mark 1:21–28

Give thanks to the LORD, invoke his name;
make known among the peoples his deeds!
Sing praise, play music;
proclaim all his wondrous deeds!
—PSALM 105:1–2

Prayers come in a host of colors including intercession, lamentation, thanksgiving, and praise. Most of us are good in the intercession department. We know how to ask for what we need. Some of us can hold our own in a lamenting contest, too. When it hurts, we cry to God about our pain, outrage, and loss. When something really wonderful comes through, we may remember to whisper a word of gratitude "upstairs." Praise, somehow, gets lost in the shuffle. How about adding a daily divine high five?

Hebrews 2:14–18
Psalm 105
Mark 1:29–39

Encourage yourselves daily while it is still "today," so that none of you may grow hardened by the deceit of sin.

—HEBREWS 3:13

Today is a big word in the Bible. You can't change the past, and you can't count on the future. Today is therefore the most important day in your life, because it's the only day in which you are free to choose. Once today is gone, there's no way in the world to get it back.

Hebrews 3:7–14
Psalm 95
Mark 1:40–45

Friday

JANUARY 16

"But that you may know that the Son of Man has authority to forgive sins on earth"—he said to the paralytic, "I say to you, rise, pick up your mat, and go home."

—MARK 2:10–11

Every time I see this miracle reenacted before my eyes, I am astonished. A man paralyzed by addictions joins AA and walks free. A woman trapped in the coffin of depression is restored to life by a healing dream. A person crushed by a cancer diagnosis finds the courage to move forward into life on new terms. Children written off as unteachable become valued and contributing members of the community. Paralysis can't hold anyone down when Jesus says, "Rise!"

Hebrews 4:1–5, 11
Psalm 78
Mark 2:1–12

JANUARY 17

• ST. ANTHONY, ABBOT •

So let us confidently approach the throne of grace to receive mercy and to find grace for timely help.

—HEBREWS 4:16

He was a wild man who fell out of love with the world and desperately in love with God. Abbot Anthony retreated farther into the desert the closer he embraced the great mystery. And the world he sought to escape followed him wherever he went, seeking his wise counsel. Anthony learned in the silence not to fear personal demons or want or God. He said, "I do not now fear God, but I love him, for love casteth fear out of doors."

Hebrews 4:12–16
Psalm 19
Mark 2:13–17

Samuel was sleeping in the temple of the LORD where the ark of God was. The LORD called to Samuel, who answered, "Here I am."

—1 SAMUEL 3:3–4

"Here I Am, Lord," by composer Dan Schutte, is one of those songs that always brings the house down. Everybody in the church feels personally charged and convicted by the refrain: "Here I am, Lord. / Is it I, Lord? / I have heard you calling in the night." I guess we've all heard that midnight call. But we're as confused as young Samuel about how to answer it, so we continue singing pointedly, "I will go, Lord / *if you lead me*" (emphasis added). That's the deal, and we're sticking to it.

1 Samuel 3:3b–10, 19
Psalm 40
1 Corinthians 6:13c–15a, 17–20
John 1:35–42

Likewise, no one pours new wine into old wineskins. Otherwise, the wine will burst the skins, and both the wine and the skins are ruined. Rather, new wine is poured into fresh wineskins.

—MARK 2:22

I wanted my adolescence to be as carefree as childhood. It wasn't. Then I expected my twenties to be as idealistic as my teens. That ship had sailed. Midlife, I wished for the shape I had when I was younger. It had melted! Now, I yearn for those healthy years when my vision was more acute and arthritis didn't nag every movement. If you spend every season of life wishing you had the old one back, don't you miss the gift of right now?

Hebrews 5:1–10
Psalm 110
Mark 2:18–22

When God made the promise to Abraham, since he had no one greater by whom to swear, "he swore by himself," and said, "I will indeed bless you and multiply" you.

—HEBREWS 6:13–14

If you can't take God at his word, who *can* you trust?
We've all known a lot of people who aren't very good
about following through on their intentions. To be honest,
we're not always as dependable as we'd like to be, either.
But when God promises to do something, it gets done.
Count on it!

Hebrews 6:10–20
Psalm 111
Mark 2:23–28

Wednesday

JANUARY 21

• ST. AGNES, VIRGIN AND MARTYR •

"Yours is princely power from the day of your birth.
In holy splendor before the daystar,
like the dew I begot you."

—PSALM 110:3

It is the rare modern teenager who aspires to be the patron
saint of chastity. That's why we need Agnes, who was no
more than thirteen when she gave up her life to preserve
her vow to God. Agnes's sacrifice astounded the Christian
world. Popes honored her grave, poets sang her praises,
and doctors of the church were humbled by her faith.
Grown-ups can talk about "just saying no." Agnes lived it
and died for it. Such purity of purpose still astonishes.

Hebrews 7:1–3, 15–17
Psalm 110
Mark 3:1–6

"To do your will is my delight;
my God, your law is in my heart!"
—PSALM 40:9

Many of us have it wrong about Old Testament law. The
Hebrew word for *law* means guiding light, not rigid rules.
Psalm 119 presents the best image: "Your word is a lamp for
my feet, a light for my path." God's law, as Moses delivered
it, is an intimate example of how God desires to share the
divine way of seeing things with a people held so close.
Divine law was never meant to be a burden. It is a gift
from lover to beloved.

Hebrews 7:25–8:6
Psalm 40
Mark 3:7–12

[He appointed the twelve:] Simon, whom he named Peter; James, son of Zebedee, and John the brother of James, whom he named Boanerges, that is, sons of thunder; Andrew, Philip, Bartholomew, Matthew, Thomas, James the son of Alphaeus; Thaddeus, Simon the Cananean, and Judas Iscariot who betrayed him.

—MARK 3:16–19

The first disciples were a curious lot. Two sets of brothers were fishermen. Matthew collected taxes. Simon the Zealot was a political agitator. Judas is called a thief in John's Gospel. Who knows how the others made their living? Today, Jesus reaches into classrooms and cubicles, truck cabs and farm fields, assembling his workforce.

Hebrews 8:6–13
Psalm 85
Mark 3:13–19

All you peoples, clap your hands;
shout to God with joyful cries,
For the LORD, the Most High, inspires awe,
the great king over all the earth.
—PSALM 47:2–3

"For beauty is never without truth, nor truth without beauty." So declared Francis de Sales, patron saint of writers. His words confirm our hunch that when we are profoundly moved by a story, a song, a sunset, grand architecture, or the trusting look in a child's eyes, we are somehow in the presence of something holy. Beauty moves us in the direction of the God who is beauty and truth itself. Make room for beauty daily.

Hebrews 9:2–3, 11–14
Psalm 47
Mark 3:20–21

When God saw by their actions how {the people of Nineveh} turned from their evil way, he repented of the evil that he had threatened to do them; he did not carry it out.

—JONAH 3:10

You and I can change God's mind. We can actually influence divine judgment and invoke divine mercy instead. Biblically, it happens all the time: Abraham dickers over the fate of Sodom in Genesis 18. Ten innocent souls would seal the deal—regrettably, God only finds four. Moses begs God not to destroy Israel for its infidelities in Exodus 32. God relents for this faithful servant. Nineveh impresses God with its repentance enough to inspire God to repent! Never underestimate the power of a converted heart.

Jonah 3:1–5, 10
Psalm 25
1 Corinthians 7:29–31
Mark 1:14–20

"If a kingdom is divided against itself, that kingdom cannot stand. And if a house is divided against itself, that house will not be able to stand."

—MARK 3:24–25

My divided heart is going to do me in. I want to serve God *and* my own interests. I strive to do the right thing but also to keep the personal cost low. I give to charity but only in moderation. All my risks for the sake of the gospel are socially acceptable and tastefully restrained. In other words, my faith doesn't impede my lifestyle at all. Deep down, I suspect that it should.

2 Timothy 1:1–8 or Titus 1:1–5
Psalm 96
Mark 3:22–30

JANUARY 27

• ST. ANGELA MERICI, VIRGIN •

I waited, waited for the LORD;
who bent down and heard my cry, . . .
And put a new song in my mouth,
a hymn to our God.
—PSALM 40:2, 4

For each of us, God composes a new song to be sung into the world. Angela Merici sang hers as a spin on "nuns as usual." When she gathered young women around her to be Ursulines, she then sent them home to remain with their families as a vital, evangelizing presence in their own network of relatives, friends, and neighbors. It was a virtual convent of the soul instead of the normal enclosure. Variations on vocations are indeed as plentiful as baptisms.

Hebrews 10:1–10
Psalm 40
Mark 3:31–35

"And some seed fell on rich soil and produced fruit."
—MARK 4:8

The seed falls on the unyielding footpath, on rocky ground, among thorns, and on rich soil. Only one will produce a harvest. Thomas Aquinas had the right kind of soil. He noted, "Prudence is knowing what to want and what not to want." It's a simple formula for spiritual success. Hungering for more stuff is not spiritually prudent. Hungering for justice is. Seeking personal glory is vanity. Giving glory to God is more honest. We can only move in the direction we're facing.

Hebrews 10:11–18
Psalm 110
Mark 4:1–20

JANUARY 29

We should not stay away from our assembly, as is the custom of some,
but encourage one another, and this all the more as you see the day
drawing near.

—HEBREWS 10:25

Who needs church? Even an introvert like me does.
I'm not a people person. But that doesn't mean I can
dispense with parish life or the Sunday assembly. Sure,
I can read my Bible at home. But I need to offer my
testimony with my presence at liturgy, and I need the
testimony of my sisters and brothers just as much. The
Body of Christ needs every last finger and toe in order to
function. We're all in there somewhere.

Hebrews 10:19–25
Psalm 24
Mark 4:21–25

"{The kingdom of God} is like a mustard seed that, when it is sown in the ground, is the smallest of all the seeds on the earth. But once it is sown, it springs up and becomes the largest of plants and puts forth large branches, so that the birds of the sky can dwell in its shade."

—MARK 4:31–32

Little Ida didn't look like much when she was a kid, believe me. The runt of the litter, she was always the least conspicuous life-form in the room. But she grew up to be a force of nature. She's now a wife to be reckoned with, a mom to depend on, a district-wide teacher of speech-impaired children, and a vigorously active member of her parish and community. Ida is, simply, indispensable. It's hard to remember she was once that irrelevant little sister of mine.

Hebrews 10:32–39
Psalm 37
Mark 4:26–34

So it was that there came forth from one man, himself as good as dead, descendants as numerous as the stars in the sky and as countless as the sands on the seashore.

—HEBREWS 11:12

"As good as dead" is familiar territory to many of us. Maybe we've been defeated in vital relationships with a spouse, parent, or child. Maybe we've given up trying to make something of our career. Maybe the artistic impulse in us has been thwarted for what seems like the last time. Maybe we've stopped believing in happiness altogether. Abraham and Sarah were once just that sure that nothing more could be expected from life. They were quite mistaken.

Hebrews 11:1–2, 8–19
Luke 1:69–70, 71–72, 73–75
Mark 4:35–41

{Moses spoke to all the people, saying:} "A prophet like me will the LORD, your God, raise up for you from among your own kinsmen; to him you shall listen."

—DEUTERONOMY 18:15

Let's talk about what Moses *didn't* say: that the prophet who arises from our own family, community, and kind is precisely the truth teller most easily ignored. The normal response of the local tribe when a prophet emerges from their midst is: "Who do you think you are, and who do you think you're talking to?" The Lorax in Dr. Seuss had better success speaking for the trees. At least the trees didn't turn him away.

Deuteronomy 18:15–20
Psalm 95
1 Corinthians 7:32–35
Mark 1:21–28

And suddenly there will come to the temple
the LORD whom you seek,
And the messenger of the covenant whom you desire.

—MALACHI 3:1

Sooner or later we all want an audience with God. Job famously demanded one. Moses climbed a mountain for his. Folks in every age fall on their knees or shake their fists and insist that God address their situation personally. But what if God grants this request, as on the day Jesus was brought to the temple? Simeon admitted he could die happy, having seen the one he waited for. Old widow Anna couldn't stop speaking about it. Would we be as glad to get what we asked for?

Malachi 3:1–4
Psalm 24
Hebrews 2:14–18
Luke 2:22–40 or 2:22–32

There was a woman afflicted with hemorrhages for twelve years. . . .
The girl, a child of twelve, arose immediately and walked around.

—MARK 5:25, 42

Here's what's known as a Marcan sandwich. The Gospel writer Mark tells two stories at once, enfolding one inside the other. A girl of twelve is dying. A woman has bled for twelve years. One is on the verge of womanhood, but it looks as though she'll never get there. The other suffers what used to be called "women's trouble," and is as good as dead to her family. Jesus demonstrates the value of womankind by drawing both back into the circle of life.

Hebrews 12:1–4
Psalm 22
Mark 5:21–43

Wednesday

FEBRUARY 4

Strive for peace with everyone, and for that holiness without which no one will see the Lord.

—HEBREWS 12:14

Some people just love a good fight. But most sane people shrink from conflict and prefer to keep the peace. Unfortunately, that impulse is not the same as actively striving for peace. As popes have insisted for generations now, peace is more than the absence of war. We can't have peace simply by preventing or subduing outbreaks of violence. The prerequisite for peace is justice; where there is injustice, there can be no peace.

Hebrews 12:4–7, 11–15
Psalm 103
Mark 6:1–6

O God, within your temple
we ponder your steadfast love.
—PSALM 48:10

Sr. Wendy is not yet a saint herself. But as an art historian, she has revealed God's steadfast love operating in the lives of the saints. In *Sister Wendy's Book of Saints,* she reminds us of how that love transformed Agatha's mutilation and martyrdom into divine aid as the patron saint of wet nurses and breast disorders. She concludes: "All who have had breast cancer will respond to her situation and her courage. They may have no choice, but neither, in her own mind, did she."

Hebrews 12:18–19, 21–24
Psalm 48
Mark 6:7–13

Jesus Christ is the same yesterday, today, and forever.
—HEBREWS 13:8

The stories of martyrs echo in every age. In 1597, the
first martyrs of the Far East took their place in the litany
of holy witnesses. In Nagasaki, twenty-six people, some
only teenagers, were crucified for their faith. The city
later devastated by the atomic bomb endured this earlier
horror as well. If the sorrow of the martyrs is always the
same, at least we can be sure the world's relentless cruelty
is matched and surpassed by the constancy of Jesus, whose
compassion never changes.

Hebrews 13:1–8
Psalm 27
Mark 6:14–29

FEBRUARY 7

When {Jesus} disembarked and saw the vast crowd, his heart was moved with pity for them, for they were like sheep without a shepherd; and he began to teach them many things.

—MARK 6:34

Lord, how often I am like those sheep, clueless and wandering dangerously along the cliffs of my life. I hope your heart is equally moved by the sight of me, making a sorry mess of my relationships, shooting off my mouth with words I can't take back, failing to cherish those whose love is dearest and best. Teach me, Lord, the things I need to know, because you are the only shepherd I trust.

Hebrews 13:15–17, 20–21
Psalm 23
Mark 6:30–34

———————

If in bed I say, "When shall I arise?"
then the night drags on;
I am filled with restlessness until the dawn.

—JOB 7:4

With everything else Job suffered, it's unfortunate to note
he was also a poor sleeper. He didn't have a clock to watch
on his dung heap, but he probably grew all too familiar
with the movement of constellations across the night sky.
He might have counted sheep, if his hadn't been destroyed
by lightning. (I'm not kidding about the sheep: see Job
1:16.) I'm a troubled sleeper too. Sometimes I wind up
reading Job. Together we make it through the night.

Job 7:1–4, 6–7
Psalm 147
1 Corinthians 9:16–19, 22–23
Mark 1:29–39

God called the dry land "the earth," and the basin of the water he called "the sea." God saw how good it was.

—GENESIS 1:10

"It's all good," my sister Evelyn often says to me at the end of a conversation. It doesn't seem to matter what we're talking about: ice cream, work, her children's latest exploits. It all winds up under the heading "good." She takes after her Creator in this regard. No matter what God produced in Genesis chapter one—time, planets, life, even gender—it all seemed pretty good to God. Some folks might say that's not very discriminating. But I find it comforting.

Genesis 1:1–19
Psalm 104
Mark 6:53–56

Tuesday

FEBRUARY 10

• ST. SCHOLASTICA, VIRGIN •

So God blessed the seventh day and made it holy, because on it he rested from all the work he had done in creation.

—GENESIS 2:3

A holy day is designed for rest. But holy living can be a lot of work! The sibling saints, Scholastica and her brother Benedict, are good examples of that. Benedict civilized Europe with his influential monasteries. Scholastica joined in his work organizing female cloisters. These twins were so close they were buried in the same grave. At their last meeting, Scholastica and her brother spoke about the joys of heaven all night long. If you find a soul mate in faith, cherish the experience.

Genesis 1:20–2:4a
Psalm 8
Mark 7:1–13

≥ 74 ≤

". . . {A} stream was welling up out of the earth and was watering all the surface of the ground. . . ."

—GENESIS 2:6

Eighteen times, Bernadette Soubirous encountered the apparition of a beautiful lady in a grotto near Lourdes in 1858. The lady called herself "the Immaculate Conception," a dogmatic statement issued by Pope Pius IX only four years earlier—hardly accessible to an illiterate fourteen-year-old like Bernadette. This young girl was also instructed to uncover the healing spring that would bring consolation to millions. People still argue about the authenticity of such visionaries. But many wish to see as Bernadette saw, and to touch the waters of new life.

Genesis 2:4b–9, 15–17
Psalm 104
Mark 7:14–23

The LORD God said: "It is not good for the man to be alone. I will make a suitable partner for him."

—GENESIS 2:18

What's a "suitable partner"? Earlier translations of this Genesis passage used the term *helpmate,* implying a subordinate position for Eve. The Hebrew text here is notoriously hard to pin down, but a less-than status is not intended. Scholar Robert Alter suggests the translation, "I will make a sustainer beside him"—a dynamic participant who benevolently intervenes on behalf of the other. Male and female, we can all use a benevolent intervention now and then.

Genesis 2:18–25
Psalm 128
Mark 7:24–30

*{Jesus} put his finger into the man's ears and, spitting, touched his
tongue; then he looked up to heaven and groaned, and said to him,
"Ephphatha!" (that is, "Be opened!")*

—MARK 7:33–34

I listen to the news. I read books. I seek counsel from
learned people as well as folks on the street. I sit in church
and pay attention during the homily. So what is it I'm not
hearing? What's the message that seems to pass me by?
Words engulf me in an endless stream of information. I'm
overwhelmed by the questions and the answers. What I'm
still listening for, I guess, is how to begin. Sweet Jesus,
open my ears to the one thing needful!

Genesis 3:1–8
Psalm 32
Mark 7:31–37

Then {God} asked, "Who told you that you were naked? You have eaten, then, from the tree of which I had forbidden you to eat!"

—GENESIS 3:11

On Valentine's Day many of us would prefer to turn our thoughts toward romance already possessed or yet to be. But as the liturgical wheel turns, we find ourselves instead attending to the first bitter story between man and woman. Both choose wrongly and blame each other for the transgression. All too often, is this not what happens to the best romances? The blame game is no way to nurture and sustain love. Take the pledge: when it comes to blame, speak only for yourself.

Genesis 3:9–24
Psalm 90
Mark 8:1–10

Sunday

FEBRUARY 15

Be imitators of me, as I am of Christ.

—1 CORINTHIANS 11:1

Imitation is the highest form of flattery, so they say. Yet why do most of us dread the hour when we recognize that we are behaving *exactly like our mothers or fathers?* This kind of imitation is on autopilot: we are destined to repeat the patterns into which we were socialized unless we deliberately choose otherwise. Think of the person you admire most, whether living or deceased. Why not consciously choose today to imitate that example?

Leviticus 13:1–2, 44–46
Psalm 32
1 Corinthians 10:31–11:1
Mark 1:40–45

*"Not so!" the LORD said to him. "If anyone kills Cain, Cain shall be
avenged sevenfold." So the LORD put a mark on Cain, lest anyone
should kill him at sight.*

—GENESIS 4:15

I've always been stunned by the protection God offers
the first murderer. We may think that a man who kills his
brother deserves no pity. Cain doesn't strike in a fit of
passion: he entertains his jealous rage, plots to waylay his
brother, and then executes his plan quite deliberately. He
then lies about it afterward. God does sentence Cain to a
heavy punishment for his crime, but will not allow him to
be struck down. Killing is evidently no answer to killing.

Genesis 4:1–15, 25
Psalm 50
Mark 8:11–13

"When I broke the seven loaves for the four thousand, how many full baskets of fragments did you pick up?" They answered [him], "Seven." {Jesus} said to them, "Do you still not understand?"

—MARK 8:20–21

Yes, Lord, I'm ashamed to admit I still don't understand. I know you multiplied loaves and fishes to feed the hungry crowds that came to hear you speak. And I believe that you are truly present in the bread and the wine of our Eucharist. I also know that our participation in this communion signals our willingness to assist you in feeding the corporal and spiritual hunger of the world. What I don't understand is: What keeps us Christians from making good on our promise?

Genesis 6:5–8; 7:1–5, 10
Psalm 29
Mark 8:14–21

Then {Jesus} laid hands on {the man's} eyes a second time and he saw clearly; his sight was restored and he could see everything distinctly.

—MARK 8:25

My friend began his entrance into blindness twice. First the lymphoma touched his eyes and caused "floaters" to dance before his vision. The doctors were able to treat this symptom and preserve his sight a while longer. But eventually, the floaters returned, and nothing could hold back the advance of the cancer. Strangely, the closer my friend moved toward blindness and death, the more distinctly he could perceive the meaning of his life. On the night before he died, he understood, loved, and forgave everything.

Genesis 8:6–13, 20–22
Psalm 116
Mark 8:22–26

FEBRUARY 19

God added: "This is the sign that I am giving for all ages to come, of the covenant between me and you and every living creature with you: I set my bow in the clouds to serve as a sign of the covenant between me and the earth."

—GENESIS 9:12–13

Covenants are promises, and the Bible is full of them: Noah is guaranteed protection from future floods; Abraham, offspring and land; Moses, God's law and abiding presence; David, an everlasting kingdom; and Jeremiah, a new and interior relationship to God. Jesus, of course, offers the "new and everlasting covenant" of his flesh and blood. Noah's covenant is unique because it's not just with humans, but with "every living creature." Do pets and houseplants go to heaven? I wouldn't be surprised.

Genesis 9:1–13
Psalm 102
Mark 8:27–33

FEBRUARY 20

Then they said, "Come, let us build ourselves a city and a tower with its top in the sky, and so make a name for ourselves; otherwise we shall be scattered all over the earth."

—GENESIS 11:4

When I finished school, I thought it was time to build myself that city with the tower in the sky. Isn't that what adulthood is *about*? One must establish a career, acquire a spouse, buy a house, fill it with children, be a good citizen, win the esteem of others, store riches in heaven on the side, and execute retirement at the proper hour with a comfortable cushion in the bank. Halfway through that plan, however, my tower fell down. Now what?

Genesis 11:1–9
Psalm 33
Mark 8:34–9:1

And {Jesus} was transfigured before them, and his clothes became
dazzling white, such as no fuller on earth could bleach them.

—MARK 9:2–3

I could see the man in the motorized wheelchair
approaching from quite a distance. His body was no
larger than a child's, his limbs contorted and spasmodic.
All I could see was the enormous suffering that must be
contained in such a reality as his. When he was close
enough for me to see his face, he smiled with a warm good
humor that spread across me like the sun appearing from
behind a cloud. Transfixed by his suffering, I almost missed
his joy.

Hebrews 11:1–7
Psalm 145
Mark 9:2–13

———————

FEBRUARY 22

Remember not the events of the past,
the things of long ago consider not;
See, I am doing something new!
—ISAIAH 43:18–19

We may feel compelled to live with our focus on the
rearview mirror, mourning lost glory or regretting old
failures. The past is often more real and more emotionally
charged than the moment we inhabit right now. But the
saving action of God is operative only in this hour. If we
want to be available to what God is doing, we have to
wake up to the present.

Isaiah 43:18–19, 21–22, 24b–25
Psalm 41
2 Corinthians 1:18–22
Mark 2:1–12

FEBRUARY 23

• ST. POLYCARP, BISHOP AND MARTYR •

The sand of the seashore, the drops of rain,
the days of eternity: who can number these?
—SIRACH 1:2

Lots of saints are known primarily for their entrance into
eternity with a spectacular death. Polycarp met his end
on a burning pyre, which alone would earn him a place in
holy memory. But more intriguingly, he was born in the
year 70 and personally knew eyewitnesses to the church's
beginnings. Polycarp's writings form a vital bridge between
the age of the apostles and the church fathers. We too
are part of the bridge between the church that is and the
church yet to be.

Sirach 1:1–10
Psalm 93
Mark 9:14–29

"If anyone wishes to be first, he shall be the last of all and the servant of all."

—MARK 9:35

The owner of the factory was a self-important man who earned a lot of snickers behind his back. Each day, he barked orders at us, but they were often disconnected to what our actual responsibilities and capabilities were. When he spoke, we nodded—and largely ignored him. Our *real* boss, the foreman, had twice the education and only a fraction of the wealth that the owner had. But he worked alongside us, assisting, encouraging, and supporting our labor. Whatever he asked, we did without question.

Sirach 2:1–11
Psalm 37
Mark 9:30–37

Wednesday

FEBRUARY 25

• ASH WEDNESDAY •

Blow the trumpet in Zion!
proclaim a fast,
call an assembly;
Gather the people,
notify the congregation. . . .
—JOEL 2:15–16

Lent starts here. Consider ourselves notified; and consider the
opportunity this season offers for recollection, repentance,
and renewal. Recollection: where are we going, and where
do we want to end up? Repentance: what aspects of our lives
need to change, and what mistakes must be acknowledged
and repaired? Renewal: what steps can we take in the next
forty days to become the people we were born to be? Praying,
fasting, and almsgiving come highly recommended.

Joel 2:12–18
Psalm 51
2 Corinthians 5:20–6:2
Matthew 6:1–6, 16–18

⇒ 89 ⇐

FEBRUARY 26

*"Here, then, I have today set before you life and prosperity,
death and doom."*

—DEUTERONOMY 30:15

Some choices are no-brainers. Life and prosperity? Sounds
great. Death and doom? No thanks! Yet when Moses set
this decision before the nation, he asked them to be most
deliberate about the direction they were about to go. It's
easy to "choose life," but harder to live out that choice in
the details. We say we choose life, and then we smoke,
eat junk that will kill us, overwork and underexercise, and
refuse to go to bed at a decent hour. Choose life—starting
with your own.

Deuteronomy 30:15–20
Psalm 1
Luke 9:22–25

FEBRUARY 27

For I know my offense;
my sin is always before me.
Against you alone have I sinned;
I have done such evil in your sight. . . .
—PSALM 51:5–6

Global warming is no longer a theory, but an increasingly uncomfortable fact of life. Science indicates that most of us will live out the rest of our lives under the consequences of the past century's choices. The decisions we make today can make possible a better future, not for us, but for our children and *their* children. Resolve to be a better steward of your resources at home, at work, and in transportation. Do it for the grandkids.

Isaiah 58:1–9a
Psalm 51
Matthew 9:14–15

If you remove from your midst oppression,
false accusation and malicious speech;
If you bestow your bread on the hungry
and satisfy the afflicted;
Then light shall rise for you in the darkness,
and the gloom shall become for you like midday. . . .

—ISAIAH 58:9–10

When the prophets start proclaiming, it's good advice. But like their original audiences, we may feel overwhelmed by all the ways they summon us to transform our attitudes. So pick one item on the prophetic menu and start there. Like "malicious speech," for example. It's easy to make the snide remark, the joke at someone else's expense, the cutting criticism behind an unsuspecting back. Speak supportively of others or not at all. Watch light rise in the darkness!

Isaiah 58:9b–14
Psalm 86
Luke 5:27–32

Sunday
MARCH 1
• FIRST SUNDAY OF LENT •

At once the Spirit drove {Jesus} out into the desert, and he remained in the desert for forty days, tempted by Satan. He was among wild beasts, and the angels ministered to him.

—MARK 1:12–13

It's a startling scene: Jesus in the desert, surrounded by beasts and angels. The humble creatures of earth and the beautiful spirits of heaven fill his days and nights in that deserted place. This image becomes a metaphor for mortal life in which we struggle with our wild, beastly selves and our angelic, better halves. Sometimes we are drawn inexorably in a beastly direction, only to be yanked back to sanity (if not sanctity) by the angels of our better nature.

Genesis 9:8–15
Psalm 25
1 Peter 3:18–22
Mark 1:12–15

"You shall not bear hatred for your brother in your heart. Though you may have to reprove your fellow man, do not incur sin because of him. Take no revenge and cherish no grudge against your fellow countrymen. You shall love your neighbor as yourself. I am the LORD."

—LEVITICUS 19:17–18

"I'm your mother, that's why." Most of us remember this argument. The line of reasoning failed to address the issue at hand but certainly defined the bottom line. Evidently Mom got it from God, who employs it liberally in the giving of the ancient law. "I am the LORD" was reason enough for the people of God to listen up. Maybe a family member or neighbor doesn't *deserve* our love or mercy, yet God insists we bear no grudge. Why? Check the bottom line again.

Leviticus 19:1–2, 11–18
Psalm 19
Matthew 25:31–46

. . . So shall my word be
that goes forth from my mouth;
It shall not return to me void,
but shall do my will,
achieving the end for which I sent it.

—ISAIAH 55:11

Dubbed "the millionaire nun," at twenty-seven Katharine Drexel inherited a fortune that she wished to bequeath to a missionary endeavor for "Indians and Colored People," as they were then called. The pope challenged her to become a missionary herself. The introverted Katharine wept at his words. She had hoped to join a cloister. Instead, she spent seventy years and twenty million dollars battling for the educational rights of Native American and African American children. Beyond comfort often lies our call.

Isaiah 55:10–11
Psalm 34
Matthew 6:7–15

For you do not desire sacrifice;
a burnt offering you would not accept.
—PSALM 51:18

Many of us daydream about how we might spend a life of privilege. What would we possess, do, and enjoy if we didn't have to work and attend to our obligations? Prince Casimir of Poland was a severe disappointment to his family when he chose to spend his short life in prayer and philanthropy. Instead of the token religious obligations expected of a prince, he chose to make a sacrifice of himself. Dying of tuberculosis at twenty-five, Casimir trusted that another kingdom awaited him.

Jonah 3:1–10
Psalm 51
Luke 11:29–32

*Queen Esther, seized with mortal anguish, likewise had recourse to the
LORD. . . . {She prayed,} "Save us by your power, and help me, who am
alone and have no one but you, O LORD."*

—ESTHER C:12, 25

"Girl power" is now fashionable in cartoons and movies,
and thank heaven for that. It always was a wasteful
proposition to write off half the human race as weak,
emotional, and prone to fainting spells in the critical hour.
Modern fathers and mothers alike desire more for their
daughters than a life of being rescued. Queen Esther is the
original teen heroine in the Old Testament. She saves the
day for her nation, with courage being the only weapon in
her arsenal.

Esther C:12, 14–16, 23–25
Psalm 138
Matthew 7:7–12

"*Therefore, if you bring your gift to the altar, and there recall that your brother has anything against you, leave your gift there at the altar, go first and be reconciled with your brother, and then come and offer your gift.*"

—MATTHEW 5:23–24

Buying your way out of guilt is a time-honored tradition. Sacrifice some grain to the gods, donate blood money to the church, slip the judge a bribe—all are variations on the same technique. Jesus calls a halt to "morality commerce" when he insists that reconciliation must come before the offering. Get your soul right first. Then write the almsgiving check!

Ezekiel 18:21–28
Psalm 130
Matthew 5:20–26

Happy those whose way is blameless,
who walk by the teaching of the LORD.
Happy those who observe God's decrees,
who seek the LORD with all their heart.

—PSALM 119:1–2

Two North African women—one pregnant, one nursing
an infant—were arrested for the crime of holding God's
power higher than any worldly empire. The *Passion of
Perpetua and Felicitas,* possibly penned by Perpetua herself, is
the stirring account of their final hours in 203. Felicity gave
birth in time to die with Perpetua. What could make these
young mothers choose to leave their infants as orphans
rather than deny their faith? They believed the greatest
legacy they could give their children was the truth.

Deuteronomy 26:16–19
Psalm 119
Matthew 5:43–48

Then Peter said to Jesus in reply, "Rabbi, it is good that we are here!
Let us make three tents: one for you, one for Moses, and one for Elijah."

—MARK 9:5

The three-tent suggestion seems pretty sensible. Here are
the two greatest authorities of Israel in conversation with
Jesus: Moses represents the great covenant of guiding law,
and Elijah the prophets of God's mighty word. Jesus is the
new miracle-working teacher. Wouldn't it be wise to hang
onto all three as long as you can? Then God weighs in:
"This is my beloved Son. Listen to him" (9:7). We listen
to Jesus because he fulfills and surpasses both law and
prophecy.

Genesis 22:1–2, 9a, 10–13, 15–18
Psalm 116
Romans 8:31b–34
Mark 9:2–10

"Stop judging and you will not be judged. Stop condemning and you will not be condemned. Forgive and you will be forgiven."

—LUKE 6:37

The order of our actions speaks volumes. Most of us are content to give charitably *after* our ship comes in. We are willing to forgive others *if* we've been recipients of their absolution. Our judgment ends *when* we ourselves have been let off the hook. But in the chess game of grace, it's always our move first. We must give freely, trusting that God will surpass us in generosity.

Daniel 9:4b–10
Psalm 79
Luke 6:36–38

Come now, let us set things right,
says the LORD:
Though your sins be like scarlet,
they may become white as snow;
Though they be crimson red,
they may become white as wool.

—ISAIAH 1:18

A young woman came to our parish seeking baptism. She wanted to be Catholic because she had had several abortions in the past, was pregnant again, and wanted to make better choices. We approached a vocal pro-life parishioner to be the woman's sponsor. The parishioner said she wasn't sure she could recommend "such a person" for baptism. Together, this unlikely pair made their journey to the Rites of Initiation at Easter. Both were transformed along the way.

Isaiah 1:10, 16–20
Psalm 50
Matthew 23:1–12

MARCH 11

My times are in your hands;
rescue me from my enemies,
from the hands of my pursuers.
—PSALM 31:16

Their grown son had a mental illness normally controlled
by medication. But he lived independently and his parents
could not protect him from unscrupulous people and
bad choices. Finally, the worst happened: he wound up
homeless, penniless, and afoul of the law in another city.
His parents had to rely on the mercy of God and the
discernment of parole officers to do right by their son.
Could those strangers see in him the good man his parents
knew was there?

Jeremiah 18:18–20
Psalm 31
Matthew 20:17–28

And {the rich man} cried out, "Father Abraham, have pity on me. Send Lazarus to dip the tip of his finger in water and cool my tongue, for I am suffering torment in these flames."

—LUKE 16:24

Dorothy Day, founder of the Catholic Worker Movement, dismissed all arguments leveled against her for providing shelter for "losers, bums, and drunks." She insisted that Christians cannot discriminate between "the 'deserving' and the 'undeserving' poor." No doubt the rich man in today's parable was aware of sore-infested Lazarus at his gate all those years, but figured that bum deserved his fate. Yet in eternity, no one questioned the integrity of Lazarus. It was the rich man's charity that was subject to judgment.

Jeremiah 17:5–10
Psalm 1
Luke 16:19–31

{Joseph's brothers} said to one another: "Here comes that master dreamer! Come on, let us kill him and throw him into one of the cisterns here; we could say that a wild beast devoured him. We shall then see what comes of his dreams."

—GENESIS 37:19–20

Jealousy is one of the seven deadly sins for a reason. It destroys marriages, divides siblings, corrodes good will in communities, and even threatens national security. When the shadow of envy falls across our hearts, we should take immediate action as if a potentially fatal virus had invaded our bodies. The only effective medicine against sin is repentance.

Genesis 37:3–4, 12–13a, 17–28a
Psalm 105
Matthew 21:33–43, 45–46

*But now we must celebrate and rejoice, because your brother was dead
and has come to life again; he was lost and has been found.*

—LUKE 15:32

The foolish younger son—with money burning a hole in
his pocket—doesn't surprise us. Nor does the outraged
older son, watching that weasel of a brother make overtures
to regain their father's affection. What does astonish us in
the story of the prodigal son is the father's willingness to
celebrate the return of a child who has done everything
wrong. The inheritance is gone for good. But the father's
love is as extravagant as ever.

Micah 7:14–15, 18–20
Psalm 103
Luke 15:1–3, 11–32

{Jesus} made a whip out of cords and drove them all out of the temple area. . . .
—JOHN 2:15

Religion has been an industry since the first primitive high priest donned vestments and earned his keep. People have made a buck off the faith of others in temple, mosque, ashram, shrine, and church ever since. Yet we can't separate out "pure" religion from the contents of our wallets altogether. Religion must not ever become simply a business. But neither can economics be viewed as a matter that does not concern the realm of faith.

Exodus 20:1–17 or 20:1–3, 7–8, 12–17 / Exodus 17:3–7
Psalm 19
1 Corinthians 1:22–25 / Romans 5:1–2, 5–8
John 2:13–25 / John 4:5–42 or 4:5–15, 19b–26, 39a, 40–42

MARCH 16

*They rose up, drove {Jesus} out of the town, and led him to the brow of
the hill on which their town had been built, to hurl him down headlong.
But he passed through the midst of them and went away.*

—LUKE 4:29–30

A prayer meeting full of irate people once tried to kill
Jesus. They were unsuccessful; he just walked away from
them. How, then, did the Sanhedrin capture him in the
end, that night in the Garden of Gethsemane? The key
to capturing Jesus was *will*—his will, that is, not that of
his enemies. Weapons were useless. A larger number of
people offered no advantage. When Jesus was ready to
lay down his life, he would. Until then, no power on
earth could stop him.

2 Kings 5:1–15a
Psalm 42
Luke 4:24–30

Deliver us by your wonders,
and bring glory to your name, O Lord. . . .
—DANIEL 3:43

Captured by pirates at sixteen! Sold into slavery in a foreign land! Sound like the screenplay for the next big action movie? It's also the true saga of Patrick, the "Apostle to the Irish." Returning as bishop to the land of his captivity, Patrick wrote, "Whatever will come my way, whether good or bad, I may accept it calmly, and always give thanks to God, who has ever shown me how I should believe in him unfailingly without end." Saint Patrick, bless us with your confidence!

Daniel 3:25, 34—43
Psalm 25
Matthew 18:21—35

Glorify the LORD, Jerusalem;
Zion, offer praise to your God. . . .
—PSALM 147:12

How does the Lenten practice of fasting offer praise to God? Eating is good, and food is plentiful; and aren't we the people of celebration after all? Fourth-century church father Cyril reminds us why we do it: "For we fast . . . not because we abhor {meals} as abominations, but because we look for our reward; that having scorned things sensible, we may enjoy a spiritual and intellectual feast." When you fast, don't work through the lunch hour. Find a quiet place for prayer, recollection, or spiritual reading.

Deuteronomy 4:1, 5–9
Psalm 147
Matthew 5:17–19

When Joseph awoke, he did as the angel of the Lord had commanded him and took his wife into his home.

—MATTHEW 1:24

He is called the man of silence. Joseph never utters one word in the Gospels. But his actions toward his wife and the son he raises as his own give eloquent witness to his faith. Joseph's obedience to God is the very definition of fidelity. When God's messenger speaks, Joseph accepts a woman with child as his wife. He moves to Egypt and back again as he is bidden. When God speaks, there isn't much left to say. Our answer is in our next decision.

2 Samuel 7:4–5a, 12–14a, 16
Psalm 89
Romans 4:13, 16–18, 22
Matthew 1:16, 18–21, 24a, or Luke 2:41–51a

Return, O Israel, to the LORD, your God. . . .

—HOSEA 14:2

The rabbis tell the story of a king and his son. The son goes astray from his father on a journey of a hundred days. His friends urge him to return, but the son, ashamed, says, "I cannot." Then the king sends word to his son: "Return as far as *you* can, and *I* will come the rest of the way." I know when I turn back at last to seek God, I only have to go halfway. God will meet me there.

Hosea 14:2–10
Psalm 81
Mark 12:28–34

> "... {F}or everyone who exalts himself will be humbled, and the one
> who humbles himself will be exalted."
>
> —LUKE 18:14

The humility thing is hard to pull off in our twenty-first-century capitalist culture. My resume is deliberately designed to be a brag fest. The only way to get ahead at my job is to announce my accomplishments early and often. In a world awash with potential awards, photo ops, and promotions, I have to let others know how valuable I am. But when I come before the Lord, I get on my knees and tell the whole truth: I'm also a sinner in need of mercy.

Hosea 6:1–6
Psalm 51
Luke 18:9–14

Sunday

MARCH 22

• FOURTH SUNDAY OF LENT •

For God did not send his Son into the world to condemn the world, but that the world might be saved through him.

—JOHN 3:17

Christianity is not in the condemning business. Jesus came to save the world, not to lose it. In fact, Jesus often reminds us not to judge unless we seek judgment for ourselves. Then how come so much religious talk points the finger, consigning whole categories of persons into the "irredeemable" pile? We Christians have our hands full proclaiming the good news of our rescue. Condemnation is a waste of words, not to mention a personally risky business.

2 Chronicles 36:14–16, 19–23 / 1 Samuel 16:1b, 6–7, 10–13a
Psalm 137
Ephesians 2:4–10 / Ephesians 5:8–14
John 3:14–21 / John 9:1–41 or 9:1, 6–9, 13–17, 34–38

Lo, I am about to create new heavens
and a new earth;
The things of the past shall not be remembered
or come to mind.

—ISAIAH 65:17

Some earlier seasons of my life provoke pleasant memories.
But not all of them. There were times of loneliness and
sadness, poor health and poor choices. I met a few people
whom, in hindsight, I would have preferred not to know.
My loved ones also suffered things I would have liked
to see them spared. For all these reasons, I eagerly look
forward to the new creation God promises. The past is
fixed, but the future is free.

Isaiah 65:17–21
Psalm 30
John 4:43–54

So the {religious leaders} said to the man who was cured, "It is the
sabbath, and it is not lawful for you to carry your mat."
—JOHN 5:10

Trust the self-righteous ones to find fault with a miracle! A
man ailing for thirty-eight years is cured at the command
of Jesus. Astonishingly, he can rise on his own volition
and has regained the strength to carry his mat. Instead of
celebrating these realities, dogmatically minded leaders
pinpoint an infraction of the Sabbath rules. I dearly wish
this were a musty old story in the coffers of religion, but,
unhappily, it's quite modern. We prefer the rules to the
people all the time.

Ezekiel 47:1–9, 12
Psalm 46
John 5:1–3a, 5–16

And the angel said to her in reply, "The holy Spirit will come upon you, and the power of the Most High will overshadow you. Therefore the child to be born will be called holy, the Son of God."

—LUKE 1:35

Nine months from today is Christmas. It's hard to think about that now, in the middle of Lent, but the church wants to remind us that even in a season of repentance, the light shines in the darkness. Liturgically speaking, Jesus may be nearing his death in Jerusalem. But in the timeless reign of God, we announce the great arrival of God with us ceaselessly.

Isaiah 7:10–14; 8:10
Psalm 40
Hebrews 10:4–10
Luke 1:26–38

{The LORD} would have decreed their destruction,
had not Moses, the chosen leader,
Withstood him in the breach
to turn back his destroying anger.

—PSALM 106:23

As the Bible often graphically illustrates, God's wrath is nothing to mess with. When God is angry, there are only two options: get out of the way if you can, and repent like crazy if you can't! Yet at the base of Mount Sinai, when the Israelites choose to worship a molten calf over the God of their very recent deliverance, Moses stands in the breach between an offended God and a dumb-as-dirt nation. Who will stand in Moses' shoes today when the nation offends?

Exodus 32:7–14
Psalm 106
John 5:31–47

To us {the just one} is the censure of our thoughts;
merely to see him is a hardship for us,
Because his life is not like other men's,
and different are his ways.

—WISDOM 2:14–15

Every saint in the church canon shares the same backstory:
he or she was impossible to live with! Some were forced
out of the communities they had founded because their
own members found them unbearable presences. Even
today, when we hear about a remarkable person, the first
thing we look for is the negating witness. Truly holy
people can seem abominable to us, because their choices
shine a flashlight in the murky corners of our own hearts.

Wisdom 2:1a, 12–22
Psalm 34
John 7:1–2, 10, 25–30

Nicodemus, one of their members who had come to {Jesus} earlier, said to {the authorities}, "Does our law condemn a person before it first hears him and finds out what he is doing?"

—JOHN 7:50–51

Only in the Gospel of John does Nicodemus make an appearance. He's not one of the Twelve, but rather a "stealth disciple" who comes to Jesus at night. And no wonder: he belongs to the Sanhedrin, and his association with Jesus might have repercussions on his career. Nicodemus appreciates the teachings of Jesus but doesn't want to pay the price of following him in broad daylight. We who abide by the Arab proverb, "Trust in God but tie your camel," certainly sympathize.

Jeremiah 11:18–20
Psalm 7
John 7:40–53

I am troubled now. Yet what should I say? "Father, save me from this hour"? But it was for this purpose that I came to this hour. Father, glorify your name.

—JOHN 12:27–28

The fourth Gospel, John, always adds a twist to the familiar story of the earlier accounts. We're used to the other three Passion narratives which contain Jesus' anguished prayer in Gethsemane: "Father, let this cup pass me by." John's more resolute portrayal of Jesus refuses this depiction of agony in the garden. Rather than showing one morsel of hesitation, John's Jesus admits to being troubled, but refuses to ask for rescue. Instead, he prays for the hour of glory—which necessarily includes his suffering.

Jeremiah 31:31–34 / Ezekiel 37:12–14
Psalm 51
Hebrews 5:7–9 / Romans 8:8–11
John 12:20–33 / John 11:1–45 or 11:3–7, 17, 20–27, 33b–45

———————

"I am completely trapped," Susanna groaned. "If I yield, it will be my death; if I refuse, I cannot escape your power."

—DANIEL 13:22

It's worth taking a few minutes today to read the whole story of Susanna and the elders from the book of Daniel. It's an all-too-familiar tale of a vulnerable woman trapped in a society that invests authority and credibility only in men. Susanna's story is still told in the voices of abuse victims who are not believed, simply because of who they are. Lord, make us all better listeners.

Daniel 13:1–9, 15–17, 19–30, 33–62 or 13:41c–62
Psalm 23
John 8:1–11

But with their patience worn out by the journey, the people complained against God and Moses, "Why have you brought us up from Egypt to die in this desert, where there is no food or water? We are disgusted with this wretched food!"

—NUMBERS 21:4–5

Complain, complain, complain. My prayers must sound wearily the same to you, Lord. I ask you to heal the ones who are sick and relieve the burden of those who are depressed. I ask for less stress, more financial security, better government, peace on earth. Multiply my prayers by the billions of people on this planet, and it must get awfully familiar. Until the world changes—until each heart changes, including mine—I can't promise anything but more of the same.

Numbers 21:4–9
Psalm 102
John 8:21–30

*If you remain in my word, you will truly be my disciples, and you will
know the truth, and the truth will set you free.*

—JOHN 8:31–32

Knowing the truth seems harder than it used to be. Or
maybe we were simply more naïve when we thought facts
were facts. If something appeared in print, it had to be
true, right? If the President said it, or a bishop, surely those
authorities could be trusted? These days, we are closer to
the gnarled "spin" in George Orwell's novel *1984* than ever
before. In the nightmare of Orwell's "Newspeak", facts
were massaged to meet the daily convenience. Jesus alone
remains the liberating truth.

Daniel 3:14–20, 91–92, 95
Daniel 3:52, 53, 54, 55, 56
John 8:31–42

Amen, amen, I say to you, whoever keeps my word will never see death.
—JOHN 8:51

The story of God's people is chock-full of promises. God makes notable covenants throughout the Bible, but none guarantee what Jesus offers: eternal life. It's the mother of all promises, because our mortality haunts us every step of our lives. Monks often made sport of the fear of death by sleeping in their coffins or, like the men of Francis of Paola's order, receiving last rites with a noose around their necks. These were visual acts of faith—death never gets the last laugh.

Genesis 17:3–9
Psalm 105
John 8:51–59

I hear the whisperings of many:
"Terror on every side!
Denounce! let us denounce him!"
—JEREMIAH 20:10

Some folks view Jeremiah as a prophet of doom. His writings do have a dark side: the word *jeremiad* came to mean any prolonged complaint or harangue. But I'm enough of a drama queen to appreciate Jeremiah's impassioned style, and I'm also conscious of his age: he was probably a teenager when God first summoned him to a career in prophecy. If his language is over the top sometimes, so is his fervor for God's justice. We might pray for his brand of commitment!

Jeremiah 20:10–13
Psalm 18
John 10:31–42

Then the virgins shall make merry and dance,
and young men and old as well.
I will turn their mourning into joy,
I will console and gladden them after their sorrows.

—JEREMIAH 31:13

When was the last time you danced? For many people, dancing is a mating ritual of youth left behind in the sobriety of adulthood. Ballroom dancers may continue to sweep across the floor into their twilight years, but the rest of us sit in chairs and tap our toes. Some even think it's inappropriate to have dancing in the Mass. But the spirit of celebration has been marked with movement since humanity's earliest memories. In the Bible, whenever God scores a victory, everybody dances.

Ezekiel 37:21–28
Jeremiah 31:10, 11-12abcd, 13
John 11:45–56

Those preceding him as well as those following kept crying out:
"Hosanna!
Blessed is he who comes in the name of the Lord!
Blessed is the kingdom of our father David that is to come!"

—MARK 11:9–10

They paid Jesus empty honors when he arrived in Jerusalem. Where were those crowds that had sung "Hosanna," just one week before? I'm in no position to judge, of course. I, too, genuflect, fold my hands, lift my hymnal, and wave my palm branches at the appropriate time. But what do these gestures mean without the total surrender of my will? What does it mean to be a disciple who surrenders nothing with my allegiance?

Mark 11:1–10 or John 12:12–16
Isaiah 50:4–7
Psalm 22
Philippians 2:6–11
Mark 14:1–15:47 or 15:1–39

Mary took a liter of costly perfumed oil made from genuine aromatic nard and anointed the feet of Jesus and dried them with her hair; the house was filled with the fragrance of the oil.

—JOHN 12:3

This scene is so sensual: how did it ever get past first-century censors? The extravagant waste of costly oil on humble feet earns a rebuke from Judas. But that's hardly the most objectionable element. What about a woman uncovering her hair in a roomful of men and using it as a towel? Mary was bucking all the conventions of religion and society in this bold action. Jesus is so impressed by her performance that he will adopt the sign of foot-washing for all disciples.

Isaiah 42:1–7
Psalm 27
John 12:1–11

*Peter said to him, "Master, why can't I follow you now? I will lay
down my life for you."*

—JOHN 13:37

Peter's words to Jesus on the night before Calvary are
painful to hear. We know where this story is headed, and
it's not in the direction of Peter making a noble choice.
In the hour of crisis, Peter does what many of us will do:
he saves himself at the expense of all other loyalties. It
will take one more phenomenal miracle for Peter—as for
us—to engage the kind of faith that allows for self-sacrifice.

Isaiah 49:1–6
Psalm 71
John 13:21–33, 36–38

Insult has broken my heart, and I am weak;
I looked for compassion, but there was none;
for comforters, but found none.

—PSALM 69:21

The worst hour of my life (so far) came in my late twenties.
All other hurts I've known in fifty years couldn't hold a
candle to that pain. I found myself physically injured,
professionally humiliated, and personally abandoned
all at the same time. If ever suffering reached biblical
proportions for me, it was that year. When psalms of
lamentation start to sound like they were written with us
in mind, we approach the threshold of understanding.
They were!

Isaiah 50:4–9a
Psalm 69
Matthew 26:14–25

*How can I repay the LORD
for all the good done for me?
I will raise the cup of salvation
and call on the name of the LORD.*

—PSALM 116:12–13

The flip side of identifying with suffering psalms (as we did yesterday) is that we should also recognize our story in psalms of gratitude. I may be able to pinpoint one clear Death Valley low moment in my life, but there have been many more mountaintop experiences. I've known love. I've seen beauty. I have felt delight bubbling up in my heart like champagne. We have a name for gratitude in Christian circles: Eucharist. It's the sacrament of those who know there's much to be thankful for.

Chrism Mass:	Evening Mass of the Lord's Supper:
Isaiah 61:1–3a, 6a, 8b–9	Exodus 12:1–8, 11–14
Psalm 89	Psalm 116
Revelation 1:5–8	1 Corinthians 11:23–26
Luke 4:16–21	John 13:1–15

Jesus answered, "You say I am a king. For this I was born and for this I came into the world, to testify to the truth. Everyone who belongs to the truth listens to my voice." Pilate said to him, "What is truth?"

—JOHN 18:37–38

The cynicism of the world has seeped into Pilate. It leaks out of him with three simple words: What is truth? The answer in John's Gospel is likewise simple: Jesus is truth. Pilate will interrogate Jesus for half the day and won't arrive at that understanding, sad to say. Nor will any of us, unless we do as Jesus recommends and listen to him.

Isaiah 52:13–53:12
Psalm 31
Hebrews 4:14–16; 5:7–9
John 18:1–19:42

As to his death, he died to sin once and for all; as to his life, he lives for God. Consequently, you too must think of yourselves as [being] dead to sin and living for God in Christ Jesus.

—ROMANS 6:10–11

What happens to Jesus happens to us. This is the message of the Easter mysteries. We aren't mere onlookers at a tragedy when we stand at the foot of the cross. We will all suffer and die. Nor are we cheering on the happy ending of an unlikely story when we stand at the tomb and hear its empty echo. We will all rise to new life. The cross is a door. Jesus walked through it so each of us could follow.

Genesis 1:1–2:2 or 1:1, 26–31a
Psalm 104 or 33
Genesis 22:1–18 or 22:1–2, 9a, 10–13, 15–18
Psalm 16
Exodus 14:15–15:1
Exodus 15:1–2, 3–4, 5–6, 17–18
Isaiah 54:5–14
Psalm 30
Isaiah 55:1–11
Isaiah 12:2–3, 4, 5–6
Baruch 3:9–15, 32–4:4
Psalm 19
Ezekiel 36:16–17a, 18–28
Psalm 42; 43 or Isaiah 12:2–3, 4bcd, 5–6 or Psalm 51
Romans 6:3–11
Psalm 118
Mark 16:1–7

On the first day of the week, Mary of Magdala came to the tomb early in the morning, while it was still dark, and saw the stone removed from the tomb.

—JOHN 20:1

No one actually saw the Resurrection. While it was arguably the most extraordinary moment in human history, there were no eyewitnesses. God chose not to make a spectacle of a miracle more astonishing than the parting of the Red Sea. All the Gospel participants get is what they leave to us: the story of an open and empty grave. This is not evidence. It is an event that requires faith. Either we believe it or we don't. And our choice makes all the difference in the world.

Acts 10:34a, 37–43
Psalm 118
Colossians 3:1–4 or 1 Corinthians 5:6b–8
John 20:1–9 or Mark 16:1–7 or, at an afternoon or evening Mass, Luke 24:13–35

{The chief priests} assembled with the elders and took counsel; then they gave a large sum of money to the soldiers, telling them, "You are to say, 'His disciples came by night and stole him while we were asleep.'"

—MATTHEW 28:12–13

Contemporary reality is an item easily bought and sold. We can't believe most of what we hear and half of what we see. Even our own experience comes to us through a heavy layer of wishful thinking, personal bias, and denial. How simple it is for politicians, news media, corporations, and others to purchase our allegiance to their assertions about the way things are. Much of the time, we want to be fooled as much as they want to snow us.

Acts 2:14, 22–33
Psalm 16
Matthew 28:8–15

Now when they heard this, they were cut to the heart, and they asked
Peter and the other Apostles, "What are we to do, my brothers?"
—ACTS 2:37

Sometimes all it takes is a poignant magazine photograph
of a suffering family in a war-torn country. At other times
it comes to us as a powerful sentence that crashes down on
us unexpectedly in the middle of a movie. The motivation
may come from the injured look in the eyes of a spouse
or child. At signature moments in our lives, we feel
charged and personally summoned to act. It's time to stop
pretending it's someone else's problem. If not us, then who?

Acts 2:36–41
Psalm 33
John 20:11–18

APRIL 15

And it happened that, while he was with them at table, he took bread, said the blessing, broke it, and gave it to them. With that their eyes were opened and they recognized him, but he vanished from their sight.

—LUKE 24:30–31

Like the travelers along the road to Emmaus, we don't really know who Jesus is until we break bread with him and share his life in the Eucharist. And until we know who Jesus is, we don't really know who we are. Or who we may be called to be.

Acts 3:1–10
Psalm 105
Luke 24:13–35

What are humans that you are mindful of them,
mere mortals that you care for them?
Yet you have made them little less than a god,
crowned them with glory and honor.

—PSALM 8:5–6

God thinks very highly of us. The phrase translated here as "little less than a god" is also rendered "just under the angels." Religious art and imagination have always portrayed angelic beings as radiantly magnificent. Not quite divine, they still belong more to heaven than to earth. The psalmist insists humanity is not far from that status in God's eyes. No wonder the church teaches that human life is sacred. If only we viewed each person with reverence for the holiness that created them!

Acts 3:11–26
Psalm 8
Luke 24:35–48

Jesus said to them, "Children, have you caught anything to eat?"
They answered him, "No."
—JOHN 21:5

The disciples of Jesus are lousy fishermen. It's one of the longest-running gags in the Gospels that they never catch a fish without divine intervention. Perhaps these men and their families would have starved by now if Jesus hadn't come along and drafted them into the service of the kingdom. Honestly, would any of us have much to show for ourselves if we, too, hadn't been included in the work of the gospel?

Acts 4:1–12
Psalm 118
John 21:1–14

Peter and John, however, said to {the leaders} in reply, "Whether it is right in the sight of God for us to obey you rather than God, you be the judges."

—ACTS 4:19

When forced to choose between the authority of God and mortals, the apostles knew which way to bow. The church still teaches that the individual informed conscience is the highest authority to which we must answer. This places a great responsibility on us to be certain our consciences are *informed*. Such a condition is reached through prayer, attentive participation in the life of the church, and thoughtful reading. Neither civic nor religious law can impel us to something we then discern to be immoral.

Acts 4:13–21
Psalm 118
Mark 16:9–15

Sunday

APRIL 19

• DIVINE MERCY SUNDAY •

Then {Jesus} said to Thomas, "Put your finger here and see my hands, and bring your hand and put it into my side, and do not be unbelieving, but believe." Thomas answered and said to him, "My Lord and my God!"

—JOHN 20:27–28

Some, like Mary Magdalene, will recognize the risen Lord when he calls them by name. Others, like the travelers on the Emmaus road, will know Jesus in the breaking of the bread. But a few will be especially blessed to see Jesus in the wounds of our sisters and brothers, and to respond with fervent faith.

Acts 4:32–35
Psalm 118
1 John 5:1–6
John 20:19–31

As they prayed, the place where they gathered shook, and they were all filled with the holy Spirit and continued to speak the word of God with boldness.

—ACTS 4:31

"You have to be there in the middle of the night to really get it," the old man whispered to me. I was on retreat at a monastery, and we were welcome to join the monks at prayer. I'm happy to pray during normal business hours—but, sorry, I don't do midnight. Still, I allowed the old man to knock on my door at some unearthly hour and lead me toward the chapel. There, by candlelight, I first experienced a room shaken by the Spirit.

Acts 4:23–31
Psalm 2
John 3:1–8

If I tell you about earthly things and you do not believe, how will you believe if I tell you about heavenly things?

—JOHN 3:12

Is the road to hell paved with good intentions? Not according to Anselm—and doctors of the church should get a hearing. Anselm insisted every action derives its value from the will behind it, since will (and not result) is within our power. "Even if we cannot fulfill our aim, yet each one will be judged before God according to his intention," Anselm concludes. Evil intent likewise will be judged against us, whether or not we succeed in it. Another reason to think heavenly thoughts!

Acts 4:32–37
Psalm 93
John 3:7b–15

And this is the verdict, that the light came into the world, but people preferred darkness to light, because their works were evil.

—JOHN 3:19

Blanche DuBois, in *A Streetcar Named Desire,* famously preferred to sit under filtered lights. The shadows flattered her advancing age and facilitated her many fictions. Integrity has the courage to present itself at midday, but lies perform best under a cover of darkness. Many of us have a shadow side that we hide from the light of truth. Confession is the best means to reveal that dark corner and to say, "This, too, is who I am, and for this I am heartily sorry."

Acts 5:17–26
Psalm 34
John 3:16–21

Thursday

APRIL 23

• ST. GEORGE, MARTYR • ST. ADALBERT, BISHOP AND MARTYR •

The LORD's face is against evildoers,
to wipe out their memory from the earth.
—PSALM 34:17

If a thing didn't happen, can it still be true? The real St.
George was a soldier martyred in Palestine during the
persecutions of 303. But he became the celebrated slayer
of dragons and rescuer of maidens in Irish legend. George
behaves the same in both stories: he uses his might for
right, protects the innocent, and wipes out evildoers. Give
or take a dragon, it's the same outcome. If our courage is
legendary, we may well become the legend.

Acts 5:27–33
Psalm 34
John 3:31–36

⇒ 147 ⇐

For if this endeavor or this activity is of human origin, it will destroy itself. But if it comes from God, you will not be able to destroy them; you may even find yourselves fighting against God.

—ACTS 5:38–39

Some sermons are better than others. But few are so bad that we would shoot the preacher. Fidelis was preaching "one faith, one Lord, one baptism" when someone took a shot at him. Timing counts here: the Protestant Reformation was in full swing. Fidelis didn't die of the bullet, which hit the wall behind him. His detractors beat him to death, however, on the way home. He forgave his murderers as he died. One rejoined the church as a result. Now *that's* effective preaching.

Acts 5:34–42
Psalm 27
John 6:1–15

The chosen one at Babylon sends you greeting, as does Mark, my son.
Greet one another with a loving kiss. Peace to all who are in Christ.
—1 PETER 5:13–14

If four witnesses in a courtroom testify alike, their testimony is pretty conclusive. Matthew, Mark, Luke, and John all wrote Gospels defending faith in Jesus. But Mark is credited with having "invented" the Gospel format that the others would imitate. Mark was not one of the Twelve, but is believed to be a companion of Peter in his old age and possibly an understudy of Paul's. Mark's testimony came first, but the Christian witness is not complete until we add our own.

1 Peter 5:5b–14
Psalm 89
Mark 16:15–20

But whoever keeps his word, the love of God is truly perfected in him.

—1 JOHN 2:5

I know my love isn't perfect. And if I ever doubt this, all I
have to do is ask those whom I love to remind me. I make
all the rookie mistakes: I'm selfish when I should be selfless,
needy instead of self-reliant, blaming in place of trusting.
I'd really like to be perfect in the service of love, but pure
love seems out of my league. Then I remember: God is the
only one who can perfect my love.

Acts 3:13–15, 17–19
Psalm 4
1 John 2:1–5a
Luke 24:35–48

So they said to him, "What can we do to accomplish the works of God?" Jesus answered and said to them, "This is the work of God, that you believe in the one he sent."

—JOHN 6:28–29

I keep thinking Christianity is more complicated than it is. I set my goals very high: follow all the rules, maintain an immaculate morality, pray hard, receive as many sacraments as humanly possible, and achieve a state of near sanctity before death. But Jesus tells his would-be disciples that the one thing—the *only* thing—they must do is put their faith in him. The works of God will be accomplished if I commit myself to this one goal.

Acts 6:8–15
Psalm 119
John 6:22–29

• ST. PETER CHANEL, PRIEST AND MARTYR • ST. LOUIS MARY DE
MONTFORT, PRIEST •

*As they were stoning Stephen, he called out, "Lord Jesus, receive
my spirit."*

—ACTS 7:59

Church father Tertullian had it right when he said, "The
blood of the martyrs is the seed of the church." Consider
the story of Peter Chanel, first martyr of the South Seas.
His initial missionary efforts on a Pacific island were so
successful that the son of the chieftain approached him for
baptism. The jealous chief had Peter slain. Within months,
the whole island was Christian. The sacrifices we make in
the name of Jesus are always repaid a hundredfold.

Acts 7:51–8:1a
Psalm 31
John 6:30–35

Jesus said to them, "I am the bread of life; whoever comes to me will never hunger, and whoever believes in me will never thirst."

—JOHN 6:35

Justice is a thirst Jesus promises to satisfy—even within the church. Women didn't join the list of church doctors until 1970. Catherine of Siena made the cut that year, as did Teresa of Ávila. (Thérèse of Lisieux was added in 1997.) Unafraid to cross wits with popes, Catherine experienced mystical visions from the age of six. The last vision, of "the ship of the church" crushing her to earth, apparently led to her death. She might be the unofficial patron of all who hope for greater recognition of female leadership in the church.

Acts 8:1b–8
Psalm 66
John 6:35–40

Thursday

APRIL 30

• ST. PIUS V, POPE •

Philip ran up and heard the {Ethiopian court official} reading Isaiah the prophet and said, "Do you understand what you are reading?" He replied, "How can I, unless someone instructs me?"

—ACTS 8:30–31

The humility of the court official is striking. He doesn't get huffy when Philip the deacon, a perfect stranger, runs up to him and asks a question that could be taken as insulting. Instead, the man shows his eagerness for learning when he invites Philip into his chariot to teach him. We are never too smart, too old, or too right to abandon the search for wisdom.

Acts 8:26–40
Psalm 66
John 6:44–51

Friday

MAY 1

• ST. JOSEPH THE WORKER •

The LORD's love for us is strong;
The LORD is faithful forever.
—PSALM 117:2

God's love is expressed sometimes in miracles, sometimes
in the ordinary. It's revealed in Mary's husband, who
resides mostly in mystery. The Gospels don't mention
Joseph after Jesus' youth. But nonbiblical sources supply
the legend of Joseph's courtship of Mary and confirm
our suspicion that raising a divine Son wasn't easy. A
fourth-century document, *History of Joseph the Carpenter*,
even supplies details of his death. But the historical Joseph
remains hidden, like the faithful of every century who live
out their love in ordinary ways.

Acts 9:1–20 / Genesis 1:26–2:3 or Colossians 3:14–15, 17, 23–24
Psalm 117
John 6:52–59 / Matthew 13:54–58

{M}any of his disciples who were listening said, "This saying is hard; who can accept it?" Since Jesus knew that his disciples were murmuring about this, he said to them, "Does this shock you?"

—JOHN 6:60–61

Some people are born to be controversial. That was true of Athanasius, who lived in a contentious age. Scholars say every heresy ever invented was alive and well in the fourth century. Athanasius took it upon himself to fight them all, thereby earning the title, "Doctor of Orthodoxy." Honors came later, however. In his lifetime, he was banished from his diocese five times and in constant need of friends in high places to reinstate him. Give a hearing to controversial figures. They may be right.

Acts 9:31–42
Psalm 116
John 6:60–69

Beloved, we are God's children now; what we shall be has not yet been revealed.

—1 JOHN 3:2

"A yellow *M*," my nephew said dreamily from the backseat during a family excursion. My sister cell phoned me to share her triumph. "We just passed a McDonald's!" she shouted. "My son is three and a half, and so far I've preserved him from the scourge of fast food. To him the Golden Arches are just a yellow *M*." The victory may be short-lived. My nephew may be happy with carrot sticks today, but what he will be—what we all will be—lies in each new decision.

Acts 4:8–12
Psalm 118
1 John 3:1–2
John 10:11–18

"But whoever enters through the gate is the shepherd of the sheep. The gatekeeper opens it for him, and the sheep hear his voice, as he calls his own sheep by name and leads them out."

—JOHN 10:2–3

Name the good shepherds in your life who have led you to be who you are today. The list may include parents, grandparents, a special aunt or uncle, and a great older sib. Teachers and coaches and mentors of every description rate a mention. Hopefully a few religious leaders make the grade. Also, heroic figures around the globe or in history books may have inspired you to choose your present course. We share a responsibility to pray for such shepherds—and to become them too.

Acts 11:1–18
Psalm 42
John 10:1–10

Tuesday

MAY 5

*So the {crowds} gathered around him and said to him, "How long
are you going to keep us in suspense? If you are the Messiah,
tell us plainly."*

—JOHN 10:24

Hearing something isn't the same as believing it. Over
and over, Jesus revealed who he was in healing signs and
teaching authority. He even came out and said he was "one
with the Father" on numerous occasions. But somehow
the people managed to translate that as "keeping us in
suspense." Of course, we too receive the extraordinary
signs of the sacraments and listen to the word proclaimed
regularly, but often live in ignorance of the divine life
within us. Go figure.

Acts 11:19–26
Psalm 87
John 10:22–30

⇒ 159 ⇐

Then, completing their fasting and prayer, they laid hands on them and sent {Barnabas and Saul/Paul} off.

—ACTS 13:3

Twenty centuries of prayer and fasting gives these actions a pretty high recommendation. And it's not just Christians who face major decisions this way—every world religion from ancient China to Native America holds the tradition of clearing the body and the mind before choosing. In Christian terms, we call such soul-searching *discernment*. More than just adding up pros and cons or flipping a coin, discernment is the task of learning the mind of God. The conclusions we reach this way often surprise us.

Acts 12:24–13:5a
Psalm 67
John 12:44–50

From Paphos, Paul and his companions set sail and arrived at Perga in Pamphylia. But John left them and returned to Jerusalem.

—ACTS 13:13

It's easy to idealize the early church. "Those were the days, when people shared their goods and loved one another," we sigh. But read between the lines and you find the humanity pretty quickly. In a puzzlingly short sentence, we learn that John Mark, cousin to Barnabas, goes home. More information about this apostolic breakup occurs in Acts 15:36–40, where Paul implies that John was a missionary wimp, and Barnabas walks away offended. The church has always been one part human, one part divine.

Acts 13:13–25
Psalm 89
John 13:16–20

Thomas said to him, "Master, we do not know where you are going;
how can we know the way?" Jesus said to him, "I am the way and the
truth and the life."

—JOHN 14:5–6

Who doesn't suffer a few existential aches and pains now
and then? These aren't the kind caused by old age; even
teenagers get them. Existential pain is suffered when the
"big questions" arise: Why am I here? What is the meaning
of my life? What am I supposed to be doing? Where
am I going, and how can I get there? Jesus is the answer
whenever life's meaning is the question. If we follow Jesus,
we'll get where we need to go.

Acts 13:26–33
Psalm 2
John 14:1–6

If you ask anything of me in my name, I will do it.
—JOHN 14:14

My friend was in midpregnancy when the doctor gave her
the difficult news. Her growing little girl had problems
that couldn't be fixed. The baby would have limited
intelligence, a malfunctioning heart, and probably would
not survive infancy. He recommended abortion. My friend
is Catholic; her husband, Muslim. They prayed together
and decided to trust in God. They now have a delightful
school-age daughter with Down syndrome. She's healthy
as a horse, eager to learn, and full of the love of life.

Acts 13:44–52
Psalm 98
John 14:7–14

When {Saul} arrived in Jerusalem he tried to join the disciples, but they
were all afraid of him, not believing that he was a disciple.

—ACTS 9:26

First impressions count, sometimes for more than they're
worth. Many of us pigeonhole our acquaintances early.
Even when people change, we often don't let the facts
challenge our preformed opinions. Saul, whose Roman
name was Paul, went from being a dangerous man to
being a disciple of Jesus in the space of an hour. But
early members of the church were still frightened of him
because of his reputation. Giving people permission to
grow is a vital part of the conversion experience.

Acts 9:26–31
Psalm 22
1 John 3:18–24
John 15:1–8

⇒ 164 ⇐

*When the crowds saw what Paul had done, they cried out in
Lycaonian, "The gods have come down to us in human form."*

—ACTS 14:11

Paul and Barnabas were the rock stars of Asia Minor. Both
were fine orators and Paul, at least, had the healing power
of the Holy Spirit at his disposal. If they wanted glory,
they could have had it in any number of towns along the
way. But what they wanted was to bring the gospel of
Jesus Christ to as many as possible. So Paul unglamorously
sewed tents for a living, and together they retained their
freedom from the tyranny of fame.

Acts 14:5–18
Psalm 115
John 14:21–26

Tuesday

MAY 12

Peace I leave with you; my peace I give to you.
—JOHN 14:27

A peaceful spirit is one sign of a genuine Christian life. We may be capable of some first-rate pretending, but peace is unusually hard to fake. It's not just about lowering your voice or your blood pressure—although those may well result from a peaceful life. Christian peace is a kind of blessed assurance that "all shall be well, and all manner of thing shall be well," as Dame Julian of Norwich wrote. It's the secret that saints and martyrs carried cheerfully to their deaths.

Acts 14:19–28
Psalm 145
John 14:27–31a

I rejoiced when they said to me,
"Let us go to the house of the LORD."
And now our feet are standing
within your gates, Jerusalem.

—PSALM 122:1–2

This psalm leaped to my lips when I got off the tour bus in honest-to-goodness Jerusalem. Many Catholics will make a pilgrimage to a holy place or shrine at some point in their lives. Israel, Assisi, and Rome are popular, as are Lourdes, Fatima, and Medjugorje. Some will prefer more local pilgrimages like the California Mission Trail or a trip to the first church in North America, the Basilica of St. Augustine in Florida. We take these journeys within us as much as outside us.

Acts 15:1–6
Psalm 122
John 15:1–8

So they proposed two {to replace Judas}, Joseph called Barsabbas, who was also known as Justus, and Matthias. Then they prayed. . . .

—ACTS 1:23–24

The would-be thirteenth apostle must have had it hard. I don't mean Matthias, who won the spiritual lottery to replace Judas among the Twelve. But what was it like for Joseph (aka Barsabbas and Justus)? The poor guy carried more IDs than an espionage agent, and still he couldn't make the cut. What was it like to be benched forever as the *apostle who never was*? The real question, of course, is, Will you and I be known as the *disciples who never were*?

Acts 1:15–17, 20–26
Psalm 113
John 15:9–17

You are my friends if you do what I command you.
—JOHN 15:14

Personally, I think anyone who works the land is a friend of God. There's something really holy about participating in the divine act of creation by bringing things to life like Isidore did and like every other farmer does. Praise God for farmers, vintners, orchardists, arborists, botanists, and small-time gardeners too. And may we never forget or forsake the migrant workers who pick the fruit and vegetables and make our food available in the markets.

Acts 15:22–31
Psalm 57
John 15:12–17

*On account of the Jews of that region, Paul had {Timothy}
circumcised, for they all knew that his father was a Greek.*

—ACTS 16:3

"Ouch," is all we can say for Timothy. Paul disliked the
practice of circumcising Gentile Christians, and he
withstood it later in the case of his assistant Titus (see
Galatians 2). Paul preached against forcing Gentiles to
behave like Jews through most of his career. Circumcising
Gentiles is like insisting that Muslims swear on a Bible—
only a whole lot more painful. Sometimes our zeal for the
forms of religion exceeds their meaning.

Acts 16:1–10
Psalm 100
John 15:18–21

This I command you: love one another.

—JOHN 15:17

Commandments are not just words of advice. Jesus is rarely as formidable about anything as he is about the love command. His tone is a far cry from sentimentality. And he's not just asking us to play nice; he expects results. Yet many of us who wouldn't dream of breaking a single precept of the church are almost cavalier about the love command. If we took this one rule seriously, we wouldn't have to worry about the rest.

Acts 10:25–26, 34–35, 44–48
Psalm 98
1 John 4:7–10
John 15:9–17

———————————

And you also testify, because you have been with me from the beginning.

—JOHN 15:27

The zeal of new Christians is exciting to be around. If you personally came into the church as an adult, have sponsored someone who has, or have witnessed adult baptisms at the Easter Vigil, you've probably absorbed the atmosphere of pure joy. Cradle Catholics might almost feel "sacrament envy" because our entry into the church happened when we were too young to appreciate it. Yet it's our testimony now that draws others to the faith we profess. That's something to be proud of.

Acts 16:11–15
Psalm 149
John 15:26–16:4a

Tuesday

MAY 19

When I cried out, you answered;
you strengthened my spirit.

—PSALM 138:3

Like all good relationships, the one between God and us
is based on a shared history. Israel sang the praises of the
One who had saved the nation many times and could be
counted on to do it again. When we pray, it's helpful to
begin by reminiscing on past occasions when God's grace
and mercy arrived right when we needed it. God doesn't
need to be reminded, of course. But we do.

Acts 16:22–34
Psalm 138
John 16:5–11

For "In him we live and move and have our being," as even some of your
poets have said, "For we too are his offspring."

—ACTS 17:28

"In him" is a popular Christian prayer formula. What we do in faith, we do in Christ. This understanding led to the inscription *IHS*—the Greek letters for the name "Jesus"—which was first adorned with a sunburst and honored by Bernardino of Siena. He believed we could attain anything through the power of the holy name if (1) we ask personally; (2) what we ask is necessary for our salvation; (3) we ask in the spirit of piety; and (4) we ask with perseverance. It's not a magic formula; it's the name above every other name.

Acts 17:15, 22–18:1
Psalm 148
John 16:12–15

So then the Lord Jesus, after he spoke to them, was taken up into heaven and took his seat at the right hand of God.

—MARK 16:19

For years I was intrigued by those Ascension paintings that show the disciples looking up at the soles of Jesus' feet as he is lost to view. Then one day I got the joke, and had to laugh at myself. Like the disciples, I was focused on the least important detail of the event. The departure of Jesus is not about saying, "Goodbye, Jesus." Instead, it is about saying, "Hello, mission of the church." If we keep looking up, we'll never get on with it.

Acts 1:1–11
Psalm 47
Ephesians 1:17–23 or 4:1–13 or 4:1–7, 11–13
Mark 16:15–20

So you also are now in anguish. But I will see you again, and your
hearts will rejoice, and no one will take your joy away from you.

—JOHN 16:22

Rita of Cascia is the patron saint of desperate situations—
about which she was all too familiar. Her husband was a
brutal and unfaithful man of whom she was relieved when
he met a violent end. She entered a convent, was known
for her piety, and is now an incorruptible—a body that
appears miraculously preserved after death (a property
generally seen with saints). The realm of anguish is still
highly populated. Rita seems determined to stay with us,
body and soul, as long as she is needed.

Acts 18:9–18
Psalm 47
John 16:20–23

{Apollos} began to speak boldly in the synagogue; but when Priscilla and Aquila heard him, they took him aside and explained to him the Way [of God] more accurately.

—ACTS 18:26

Thank you, God, for all who have participated in my education so far. Thank you for teachers and professors in formal classrooms who opened worlds for me with their patient instruction. Thank you for talented preachers and wise spiritual directors. I'm especially grateful for friends who took the risk of correcting me when I was wrong about relationships, attitudes, and ideas. Even if it hurt or offended me, I see now that it would have hurt much worse to move forward with my faults.

Acts 18:23–28
Psalm 47
John 16:23b–28

No one has ever seen God.

—1 JOHN 4:12

Who am I to doubt Scripture? Still I suspect more of us have seen God than has been officially recorded. The ancient woman I saw standing in her rose garden, with her beatific smile—surely that was God. The man begging on the street corner and tipping his hat to all who contributed to his cup—God again. The child in the photo who lost limbs to a land mine from a war that adults are no longer fighting—God too, no doubt. God has so many faces.

Acts 1:15–17, 20a, 20c–26
Psalm 103
1 John 4:11–16
John 17:11b–19

• ST. BEDE THE VENERABLE, PRIEST AND DOCTOR OF THE CHURCH •
ST. GREGORY VII, POPE • ST. MARY MAGDALENE DE' PAZZI, VIRGIN •
MEMORIAL DAY •

I have told you this so that you might have peace in me.

—JOHN 16:33

Someone said that world peace begins when patience
is exercised on the personal level. We have lots of
opportunities to practice this as we sit in gridlock, queue
up in checkout lines, or wait on news that's slow to arrive.
Venerable Bede whimsically noted that we pray frequently,
Thy kingdom come, and yet "nevertheless we are not going
to receive the kingdom as soon as our prayer is finished,
but at the proper time." Some of us are content to wait on
this one.

Acts 19:1–8
Psalm 68
John 16:29–33

Tuesday

MAY 26

• ST. PHILIP NERI, PRIEST •

I served the Lord with all humility. . . .
—ACTS 20:19

The lore of saints fell out of favor in the last generation,
perhaps because so many stories about them traded on
the currency of suffering and dying. Those were popular
themes in the Middle Ages but less so in the boom years
following the Second World War. But among the saints are
also found folks like Philip Neri, remembered mostly for
his personal warmth, gaiety, and gentleness. He also had a
self-deprecating wit as he prayed, "Lord, watch Philip: he
will betray you!" Self-knowledge begets humility.

Acts 20:17–27
Psalm 68
John 17:1–11a

Wednesday

MAY 27

*They were all weeping loudly as they threw their arms around Paul
and kissed him, for they were deeply distressed that he had said that
they would never see his face again.*

—ACTS 20:37–38

"Parting is such sweet sorrow." So Romeo bids his Juliet
goodbye in Shakespeare. And so Christians bid each other
farewell, especially at the long goodbye of death. Many
of us have had to let go of parents, sisters and brothers,
children, and longtime friends. The sorrow is deep and
real. But the sweetness is also real: born of our faith in the
resurrection that awaits us. We only say goodbyes in a
world that is also passing.

Acts 20:28–38
Psalm 68
John 17:11b–19

⇒ 181 ⇐

I keep the LORD always before me;
with the Lord at my right, I shall never be shaken.
—PSALM 16:8

The faith of my friends continues to challenge me. Lou's wife left for reasons that had little to do with him. He healed and found the courage to love again. Anne's grown son died not long after his wedding day. She continues to be a woman of hope. John has borne much rejection because of his homosexuality, but he remains welcoming, loving, and kind. Phyllis lost her eyesight, but not her sense of humor. Lord, teach me to see you as they do.

Acts 22:30; 23:6–11
Psalm 16
John 17:20–26

Jesus said to Simon Peter, "Simon, son of John, do you love me more than these?"

—JOHN 21:15

On my best days, I might have answered Jesus like Peter did, with fervent commitment. On other days, I fear I would have said this: "Yes, Lord, I love you. Quite a lot; but let's be reasonable. One has responsibilities. Things cost money. You can't expect miracles. You have to live in the real world. Nobody will take care of you if you don't take care of yourself." And then I would have hid from Jesus like Peter once did and wept bitterly.

Acts 25:13b–21
Psalm 103
John 21:15–19

There are also many other things that Jesus did, but if these were to be described individually, I do not think the whole world would contain the books that would be written.

—JOHN 21:25

A Holocaust survivor broke down during an interview about the atrocities she experienced in the concentration camps. "So many stories," she murmured. "If you had all the pens and all the paper in the world, you could not write them down." Human history is full of horror, and we would be wise to record it faithfully. But we must also remember the record of wonder that accompanies us, and how every step and every breath is a miracle.

Acts 28:16–20, 30–31
Psalm 11
John 21:20–25

And suddenly there came from the sky a noise like a strong driving
wind, and it filled the entire house in which they were.

—ACTS 2:2

A driving wind. A gift of fire. Courage reborn. And the last
gift of Pentecost is perhaps the most surprising one: the
power of language. In a world hopelessly divided by race
and nationality, as well as ideology and economics, there
comes a speech that has the ability to unite and to heal.
That tongue is rarely spoken in history, but it could be.

Acts 2:1–11
Psalm 104
1 Corinthians 12:3b–7, 12–13 or Galatians 5:16–25
John 20:19–23 or John 15:26–27; 16:12–15

I, Tobit, have walked all the days of my life on the paths of truth and righteousness.

—TOBIT 1:3

Treat yourself to a great story. The book of Tobit is a featured reading this week, and we'll be dipping daily into this fairy-tale-like novella. Tobit is like Job: a thoroughly good fellow who suffers innocently. But the story revolves around his son Tobias, who keeps company with an angel and has to face a killer demon. Goodness wins, love happens, and old Tobit gets the cure he needs. Human history is rarely like the story of Tobit—but eternity will be. So we believe.

Tobit 1:3; 2:1a–8
Psalm 112
Mark 12:1–12

Is it lawful to pay the census tax to Caesar or not? Should we pay or
should we not pay?
—MARK 12:14

The relationship between God and Caesar was uneasy
from the start. Jesus recommends we honor both according
to their respective authorities. But what about where their
jurisdiction overlaps, as it does when economic issues
become moral ones? I want to support roads and schools
and health coverage for the disadvantaged. I don't want to
contribute to global warming, wars of aggression, capital
punishment, or abortion. My tax dollars are spent in ways I
don't personally control. Trusting Caesar to do God's will
is a questionable business.

Tobit 2:9–14
Psalm 112
Mark 12:13–17

In you I trust; do not let me be disgraced;
do not let my enemies gloat over me.
—PSALM 25:2

Fifteen boys chose to be burned alive with Charles Lwanga
in nineteenth-century Uganda. The boys were court pages
who were sexually abused by their powerful chieftain.
Lwanga, only twenty-six himself, was in charge of the boys
when another Catholic accused the chieftain of the abuse.
In retaliation, Catholicism was put on trial, and Lwanga
and the boys were told to renounce their faith or die for it.
Our youth continue to need patrons as fearless as Charles
to stand with them.

Tobit 3:1–11a, 16–17a
Psalm 25
Mark 12:18–27

Your marriage to her has been decided in heaven! Take your kinswoman; from now on you are her love, and she is your beloved.

—TOBIT 7:11

A marriage made in heaven? In Tobit, the union of Sarah and Tobias seems to originate farther south. The bride has a demon that has slain seven husbands so far. Tobias's new father-in-law will slip out shortly to dig his grave. Yet these words turn out to be prophetic. God has an eye on this marriage and intends to bring good out of it. Before we give up on any couple, we might pray for an angel to chase the devil out of their union.

Tobit 6:10–11; 7:1bcde, 9–17; 8:4–9a
Psalm 128
Mark 12:28b–34

Praise the LORD, my soul;
I shall praise the LORD all my life,
sing praise to my God while I live.

—PSALM 146:2

Praising the *right* God can be crucial. The great oak tree
of Thor had stood near Fritzlar for ages. The Norse god
of thunder commanded the weather and the harvest, so
people revered this tree. When Boniface came to town to
proclaim the gospel, no one would listen. They trusted
in Thor. So Boniface cut down the mighty oak—and he
wasn't struck by lightning! Conversions followed. If we
plant a false hope dead center in our lives, it must fall
before we can embrace the truth.

Tobit 11:5–17
Psalm 146
Mark 12:35–37

A king's secret it is prudent to keep, but the works of God are to be declared and made known.

—TOBIT 12:7

God's works are to be shouted out loud. But God also likes to work in mysterious ways. St. Boniface drew converts because the god of thunder didn't smite him (see yesterday). By comparison, St. Norbert came to faith because he was imperiled during a thunderstorm. The formerly high-living prince was startled into spiritual wakefulness by his near-death experience. God is prepared to use any power, natural or supernatural, to get our attention. We would make it easier on ourselves if we'd just come quietly.

Tobit 12:1, 5–15, 20
Tobit 13:2, 6efgh, 7, 8
Mark 12:38–44

*Go, therefore, and make disciples of all nations, baptizing them in the
name of the Father, and of the Son, and of the Holy Spirit. . . .*

—MATTHEW 28:19

God our Creator, we praise you for the beauty, the wonder,
and the mystery we encounter in the world you made for
our delight. Jesus our Redeemer, we praise you for the gift
of our grand rescue from sin and death. Spirit of holiness,
we praise you for the sacrament of each day, which breaks
open to show us the goodness of God.

Deuteronomy 4:32–34, 39–40
Psalm 33
Romans 8:14–17
Matthew 28:16–20

Blessed are the merciful,
for they will be shown mercy.
—MATTHEW 5:7

My friend Dale was the sort of guy who took pity on every suffering creature, large and small. He once found a newborn fawn whose mother had been killed. He nursed it with a baby bottle, and that deer followed him around like a dog for years. Dale was the same way with children, the homeless, neurotics, drunks, and fools. Then Dale suffered a brain hemorrhage that robbed him of speech and mobility. The whole darn world poured in to care for him.

2 Corinthians 1:1–7
Psalm 34
Matthew 5:1–12

Steady my feet in accord with your promise;
do not let iniquity lead me.

—PSALM 119:133

Doctors of the church are all doctors of *something*. They each have a special patronage: the composer Ephrem is the "Doctor of Deacons and Poets." To Ephrem, hymns weren't just traveling music to get us in and out of Mass and up to communion. They were weapons in the fight against heresy. He prayed before he wrote, so that his work would be consecrated to God's purposes. It's a great way to get more than a paycheck for our labors.

2 Corinthians 1:18–22
Psalm 119
Matthew 5:13–16

Not that of ourselves we are qualified to take credit for anything as coming from us; rather, our qualification comes from God. . . .
—2 CORINTHIANS 3:5

We hear a lot about *self-made* people. It's quite a trick, since we all come from two parents and a long line of genetic material. But as significant as genes are, biology alone is not our destiny. A host of teachers and heroes— and even opponents and obstacles—participate in our formation. Social factors and personal choices also join the mix. Above all, existence itself has divine origins. Whatever we make of ourselves is ultimately a return on God's investment.

2 Corinthians 3:4–11
Psalm 99
Matthew 5:17–19

Then {Barnabas} went to Tarsus to look for Saul, and when he had found him he brought him to Antioch. . . . and it was in Antioch that the disciples were first called Christians.

—ACTS 11:25, 26

Often I meet characters in the Bible I want to know better. But they glide in and out of the story without leaving more than a calling card. Barnabas is one of those. At a time when no one wanted to trust killer-turned-disciple Paul of Tarsus, Barnabas risked being his sponsor. From his decision, the whole future of the church would take shape. May we all learn to read the movement of the Spirit with such discernment!

Acts 11:21b–26; 13:1–3
Psalm 98
Matthew 5:20–26

But we hold this treasure in earthen vessels, that the surpassing power may be of God and not from us.

—2 CORINTHIANS 4:7

My earthen vessel is getting a little leaky nowadays. The hair's gone grey, the limbs creak and ache, and the memory is not as reliable as it used to be. One glance in the mirror reminds me I'm not Julia Roberts, or even her older sister. And a good examination of conscience reminds me I'm also not Mother Teresa. Whatever goodness, beauty, or truth comes from me has its origins in the God who made me. I'm just the caretaker here.

2 Corinthians 4:7–15
Psalm 116
Matthew 5:27–32

JUNE 13

• ST. ANTHONY OF PADUA, PRIEST AND DOCTOR OF THE CHURCH •

*And all this is from God, who has reconciled us to himself through
Christ and given us the ministry of reconciliation. . . .*

—2 CORINTHIANS 5:18

Imagine spending your afterlife gathering lost socks and
misplaced keys! Anthony of Padua is more than just the
go-to guy for lost items. As "Doctor of Evangelism," he
is considered one of the finest preachers the church ever
produced. Anthony urged that our compassion should
be like God's: "gracious, spacious, and precious." By this
he meant that divine mercy transforms us with its grace,
encompasses us with its abundance, and leads to eternal
joy. Put this threefold compassion into practice.

2 Corinthians 5:14–21
Psalm 103
Matthew 5:33–37

While they were eating, he took bread, said the blessing, broke it, and gave it to them, and said, "Take it; this is my body."

—MARK 14:22

A good preacher once brought to my attention the four actions of the Eucharist: Jesus *took, blessed, broke,* and *gave* his Body and his Blood. In turn, Jesus was taken and broken in the violent movements of his Passion. Yet he responded with blessing and giving from the cross. The consecration represents an unholy violence transformed into a blessing for the human race. We celebrate and pledge to participate in this transformation with our lives in every Eucharist.

Exodus 24:3–8
Psalm 116
Hebrews 9:11–15
Mark 14:12–16, 22–26

———————————

Behold, now is a very acceptable time; behold, now is the day of salvation.

—2 CORINTHIANS 6:2

Today's the day of God's great rescue! Still, I'm putting off reforming my life until tomorrow. I need more time to do it right, and a clearer head to think things through. I've got relationships to reconcile, forgiveness to give and to ask for. I've got bad habits to change and judgment-free attitudes to adopt. There's work to be done, and I'll be the first to admit it. And I'll get right on it tomorrow. Too bad the acceptable timetable is "now."

2 Corinthians 6:1–10
Psalm 98
Matthew 5:38–42

JUNE 16

You have heard that it was said, "You shall love your neighbor and hate your enemy." But I say to you, love your enemies. . . .

—MATTHEW 5:43–44

Without warning, the rain poured down. Joanna and I dashed into the nearest doorway for cover. We were not friends. We were antipathies: those with a natural aversion to each other. Joanna and I had been unwilling roommates locked in a contest of wills since the day we met. But now we were trapped together in a narrow doorway. "You don't like me," she said frankly. "And I'm not wild about you. So what should we do about this?" In that hour, we tried friendship.

2 Corinthians 8:1–9
Psalm 146
Matthew 5:43–48

Each must do as already determined, without sadness or compulsion, for God loves a cheerful giver.

—2 CORINTHIANS 9:7

I took a course called Ministry 101. Enrolled in the class were future priests, missionaries, religious, and lay workers of the church. We were each asked to explain why we felt a vocation to ministry. So we spoke passionately and at length about the great need of the world that weighed on our hearts, the terrible injustices that shamed us, the anger we experienced at the suffering of humanity. Our teacher listened. Finally, she asked, "Anybody here out of love?"

The room grew silent.

2 Corinthians 9:6–11
Psalm 112
Matthew 6:1–6, 16–18

In praying, do not babble like the pagans, who think that they will be heard because of their many words. Do not be like them. Your Father knows what you need before you ask him.

—MATTHEW 6:7–8

God, it's me. So you know what I'm asking for, again. Same petition, different day. But this time, I come to you with a new heart.

2 Corinthians 11:1–11
Psalm 111
Matthew 6:7–15

I drew them with human cords,
with bands of love. . . .
—HOSEA 11:4

Catholics of a certain age grew up with a picture of the
Sacred Heart hanging on the wall. The eyes followed us
around the room while the heart burned without being
consumed. We may have wondered how a heart could
be on fire that way: with love, with grief, with suffering.
Later on, we learned more about love, grief, and suffering
ourselves. And we found ourselves in communion with the
heart of Christ at last.

Hosea 11:1, 3–4, 8c–9
Isaiah 12
Ephesians 3:8–12, 14–19
John 19:31–37

And he said to them, "Why were you looking for me? Did you not know that I must be in my Father's house?" He went down with them and came to Nazareth, and was obedient to them; and his mother kept all these things in her heart.

—LUKE 2:49, 51

If the heart of Jesus is characterized by its fiery passion, the heart of Mary is known for its inviolable purity. The average heart, by contrast, is remarkable mostly for its checkered makeup. We serve many masters, and we kneel before many altars, some holy, some quite pagan and foreign to what we say we believe. Mary, our mother, has a heart magnificently uncluttered by the debris of rival affections. She is happy to lead her children to a simpler way of loving.

2 Corinthians 12:1–10
Psalm 34
Luke 2:41–51

{Jesus} woke up, rebuked the wind, and said to the sea, "Quiet! Be still!" The wind ceased and there was great calm. Then he asked them, "Why are you terrified?"

—MARK 4:39–40

A short list of reasons why I live in fear: I doubt myself. I know I can't earn the love that's shown to me. I suspect my success so far is a mirage. I think I'm a phony in certain crucial ways. I'm not sure there will ever be enough money. My body is falling apart by perceptible degrees. My wrongs outweigh my charitable deeds. I don't think I'm good enough to get to heaven.

One reason not to fear: God's promises.

Job 38:1, 8–11
Psalm 107
2 Corinthians 5:14–17
Mark 4:35–41

Monday

JUNE 22

• ST. JOHN FISHER, BISHOP AND MARTYR • ST. THOMAS MORE, MARTYR •
ST. PAULINUS OF NOLA, BISHOP •

I will make your name great,
so that you will be a blessing.
— GENESIS 12:2

Layman Thomas More is familiar to us in the movies as the
unyielding and immovable "man for all seasons." Imprisoned
along with More, Bishop John Fisher was a less flintlike
person in his political stance. A moderate thinker during
the Reformation, Fisher opposed Martin Luther too but
was sympathetic to the need for church reform. We think
of martyrdom as the special fate of those with unbending
principles like More's. Moderates, too, die for what they
believe. Conviction is the starting point of all heroism.

Genesis 12:1–9
Psalm 33
Matthew 7:1–5

Do to others whatever you would have them do to you. This is the law and the prophets.

—MATTHEW 7:12

If I really intended to treat others as I want to be treated, here's what I'd do. I'd give people the benefit of the doubt. I would presume they had the best intentions at heart, even when those weren't in evidence. I'd forgive folks when they screwed up, and speak well of them in their absence. I'd be happy to see them whenever they showed up, even if it wasn't convenient. Anyone would be welcome at my table. Isn't the Golden Rule worth a shot?

Genesis 13:2, 5–18
Psalm 15
Matthew 7:6, 12–14

Though I thought I had toiled in vain,
and for nothing, uselessly, spent my strength,
Yet my reward is with the LORD,
my recompense is with my God.

—ISAIAH 49:4

Who was John the Baptist? His baptisms were spectacular
events, but forgotten in short order. He had disciples, some
of whom deserted him for the next big thing. John went
to prison, and was beheaded at the whim of an offended
queen. His following collapsed within a generation or two.
Overall, John was not a particularly fruitful leader. But he
anticipated that outcome, insisting he would decrease to
make room for someone greater. His greatest achievement,
then, was his astonishing humility.

Vigil:	Day:
Jeremiah 1:4–10	Isaiah 49:1–6
Psalm 71	Psalm 139
1 Peter 1:8–12	Acts 13:22–26
Luke 1:5–7	Luke 1:57–66, 80

Not everyone who says to me, "Lord, Lord," will enter the kingdom of heaven, but only the one who does the will of my Father in heaven.

—MATTHEW 7:21

We know that acquiring *religion* is not the goal of our faith. Christianity is not about going to church, participating in rituals, saying prayers, or being spiritual. It's not about collecting six of the seven sacraments before we die. Having pious attitudes or being knowledgeable about the holy stories is not enough. Even being good and not breaking the rules doesn't earn us salvation. Uniting our will with God's will is more like it. That takes time, not to mention grace.

Genesis 16:1–12, 15–16 or 16:6b–12, 15–16
Psalm 106
Matthew 7:21–29

Then Abraham said to God, "Let but Ishmael live on by your favor!"
—GENESIS 17:18

God's grace is making its purposeful way through history.
Where it finds a willing heart, it makes a home among
us. Unfortunately, we often make plans that confound
the natural flow of grace. So Abraham and Sarah, tired of
waiting for God to supply them with the promised heir, try
an ancient route to parenthood through Hagar, who bears
Ishmael. As always, God incorporates our every detour into
the plan. The route to salvation is still through Isaac, yet
Ishmael gets his blessing too.

Genesis 17:1, 9–10, 15–22
Psalm 128
Matthew 8:1–4

You may go; as you have believed, let it be done for you.
—MATTHEW 8:13

You and I missed the great theology wars where "what we believe" was fought and won. The church concluded those by the fifth century. Of course, the Great Schism in 1054 would result in the separation of Eastern (Orthodox) and Western Christianity. The Protestant Reformation of the 1500s would likewise lead to further battles. But Cyril of Alexandria, the fourth-century "Doctor of the Incarnation," settled "the big one": the humanity and divinity of Jesus. Jesus, Son of God and our brother, make your church one family.

Genesis 18:1–15
Luke 1:46–47, 48–49, 50, 53, 54-55
Matthew 8:5–17

God did not make death,
nor does he rejoice in the destruction of the living.

—WISDOM 1:13

We learn about death early. It's never an easy lesson. The firefly fails in the jar after we took such care to punch holes in the lid. The baby bird falls from its nest, and we're helpless to redeem the loss. When a beloved grandparent is buried, the season of death begins in earnest. We start to sense that death is inescapable, not merely a rare tragedy but an inevitable reality. This knowledge changes everything. For people of faith, the Resurrection, too, changes everything.

Wisdom 1:13–15; 2:23–24
Psalm 30
2 Corinthians 8:7, 9, 13–15
Mark 5:21–43 or 5:21–24, 35b–43

Monday

JUNE 29

• ST. PETER AND ST. PAUL, APOSTLES •

I have competed well; I have finished the race; I have kept the faith.
—2 TIMOTHY 4:7

Holy apostles Peter and Paul, you are the twin poles in
the life of the church. Peter, you conserve the wisdom and
the truth of the tradition; Paul, you insist that old forms
must consider new realities. Guard the church you helped
inaugurate and guide us, in every age, to remember the
lessons you taught together at such a price.

<table>
<tr><td align="center">**Vigil:**</td><td align="center">**Day:**</td></tr>
<tr><td align="center">Acts 3:1–10</td><td align="center">Acts 12:1–11</td></tr>
<tr><td align="center">Psalm 19</td><td align="center">Psalm 34</td></tr>
<tr><td align="center">Galatians 1:11–20</td><td align="center">2 Timothy 4:6–8, 17–18</td></tr>
<tr><td align="center">John 21:15–19</td><td align="center">Matthew 16:13–19</td></tr>
</table>

Test me, LORD, and try me;
search my heart and mind.
Your love is before my eyes;
I walk guided by your faithfulness.

—PSALM 26:2–3

Tyrants wreak their cruelty in every age. When two-thirds
of the city of Rome burned in the year 64, Emperor Nero
supplied a scapegoat in the Christian population. The
upper class suspected that Nero himself set the fire, but
prejudice in the streets was easy to direct at the already
hated Christians. Peter, Paul, and countless others perished
in Nero's "garden party," bordered by human torches,
crucifixions, and other atrocities. Yet the Christian witness
continues to set the world on fire, one life at a time.

Genesis 19:15–29
Psalm 26
Matthew 8:23–27

{N}o one could travel by that road.
—MATTHEW 8:28

Fancy yourself a born traveler? Junípero Serra probably had you beat by a mile—650 miles to be exact. That's how long "The Royal Road," El Camino Real, stretches between San Diego and Sonoma. The California Mission Trail established by Serra was meant to encompass three missions originally, but Serra decided to build one at the end of every good day's walk, which resulted in twenty-one missions altogether. Not all survive, but take the pilgrimage sometime and see these gorgeous holy spaces. Feel free to rent a car!

Genesis 21:5, 8–20a
Psalm 34
Matthew 8:28–34

Then God said: "Take your son Isaac, your only one, whom you love, and go to the land of Moriah. There you shall offer him up as a {burnt offering} on a height that I will point out to you."

—GENESIS 22:2

No one knows why God might ask of Abraham the death of his child. Nor can anyone explain why children are lost daily to hunger and thirst, war and violence, illness and accidents, in countries around the world. Such hard realities threaten to crush us every time they overtake us, even when we know they play no part in God's will. We look to the cross, where God's own son hangs dying. God is no stranger to our grief.

Genesis 22:1b–19
Psalm 115
Matthew 9:1–8

But {Thomas} said to them, "Unless I see the mark of the nails in his hands and put my finger into the nailmarks and put my hand into his side, I will not believe."

—JOHN 20:25

Some things aren't real to me until I touch them. My latest out-of-state niece isn't born for me until I hold her in my arms. The holiday feast doesn't quite begin until I lift the first forkful to my mouth. I don't believe in vacation until I've got a suitcase and a ticket in hand. Jesus doesn't fault Thomas, or us, for being slow to grasp an abstract truth. That's why we have sacraments, so we can touch the mysteries of God one by one.

Ephesians 2:19–22
Psalm 117
John 20:24–29

"People do not put new wine into old wineskins. . . . Rather, they pour new wine into fresh wineskins, and both are preserved."
—MATTHEW 9:17

When the United States of America came into being, it definitely qualified as a new wine in a fresh wineskin. The former colonists had bold ideas about how to be citizens unencumbered by king and pope alike. Government would be different here. Worship would be freer, too. U.S. citizens might expect to escape every fetter short of death and taxes! It was a grand proposal, freedom. But with it comes a heightened responsibility that each of us must bear alone.

Genesis 27:1–5, 15–29
Psalm 135
Matthew 9:14–17

Sunday
JULY 5

As {the LORD} spoke to me, spirit entered into me and set me on my feet. . . .
—EZEKIEL 2:2

You've had this experience. You're sitting in church, mind adrift, the words of the liturgy swirling around you like a comfortable fog. It's not that you're not interested; it's just the interior buzz that's causing the usual distraction. What is it you're doing later today? Just then, a phrase from outside penetrates the fog and pierces your heart, capturing your attention. What was that? Did God just say something—*to me?* How shall I respond to this? What will it cost if I do?

Ezekiel 2:2–5
Psalm 123
2 Corinthians 12:7–10
Mark 6:1–6

⇒ 220 ∈

Jesus turned around and saw her, and said, "Courage, daughter! Your faith has saved you."

—MATTHEW 9:22

Some of us were mistaught the lesson of little Maria Goretti's life. She died in 1902 at the age of twelve, murdered by a young man during an attempted rape. In my generation, Maria was upheld for her perfect chastity. This sounds wrong: do we want our daughters to believe their virginity is more valuable than their lives? Yet Maria's amazing achievement was to forgive her attacker before she died. Rescued from darkness, the man attended her canonization in 1950.

Genesis 28:10–22a
Psalm 91
Matthew 9:18–26

The man then said, "Let me go, for it is daybreak." But Jacob said, "I will not let you go until you bless me."

—GENESIS 32:27

Most of us, like Jacob, have wrestled from time to time with the angels of our better natures. We strive against them, struggling to break free from their influence. But those old lessons go deep: all the Catholic school years, Sunday homilies, days of recollection or examination of conscience, the sterling examples of the saints. We've heard the gospel stories too many times to pretend that we don't get it. James Joyce said it best: "There are no ex-Catholics; only lapsed ones."

Genesis 32:23–33
Psalm 17
Matthew 9:32–38

Give thanks to the LORD on the harp;
on the ten-stringed lyre offer praise.

—PSALM 33:2

Note to the psalmist: I've misplaced my harp. And where's
that lyre when you need it? Oh well, I can give thanks to
God in inventive ways. I'll stand at the window, gratefully
watching the blessed summer rain pour down, relieving this
awful humidity. I'll praise God with a slice of pie, savoring
each bite instead of eating absentmindedly, missing the
pure gift of food. I'll even praise God with my checkbook,
sending something along to my favorite mission. It's all
music to God's ears.

Genesis 41:55–57; 42:5–7a, 17–24a
Psalm 33
Matthew 10:1–7

• ST. AUGUSTINE ZHAO RONG, PRIEST AND MARTYR, AND HIS
COMPANIONS, MARTYRS •

*As you go, make this proclamation: "The kingdom of heaven is
at hand."*

—MATTHEW 10:7

It's easy to forget about the church in China, since
Chinese Catholics who don't accept the government-
approved parishes with state-appointed bishops have
been underground for a generation. Ten million Chinese
Catholics are still working toward religious liberty. Father
Zhao Rong was 1 of 120 known Chinese citizens to die for
the faith between 1648 and 1930. Yet the church in China
is still not free, and needs our prayers every day.

Genesis 44:18–21, 23b–29; 45:1–5
Psalm 105
Matthew 10:7–15

There God, speaking to Israel in a vision by night, called, "Jacob!
Jacob!" "Here I am," he answered.

—GENESIS 46:2

Characters in the Bible have this way of popping up and
declaring themselves ready to be enlisted in God's latest
scheme—even before they know what it is. When I hear
God calling *my* name, I'm more likely to reply, "Nobody
here but us chickens." What would it take to shout,
cheerily, "Here I am!"

Genesis 46:1–7, 28–30
Psalm 37
Matthew 10:16–23

Sing praise, play music;
proclaim all {God's} wondrous deeds!
—PSALM 105:2

"Idleness is the enemy of the soul," according to the
Rule of St. Benedict, which has been governing Western
monasteries for fifteen centuries. You don't have to be a
monk to know how true this is. Even when we are caught
up in the frenzy of modern busyness, pockets of dead time
do wind up in our meticulously scheduled days. As they
say of superheroes, "This power can be used for good or
evil." For such times, keep a book of psalms in the glove
compartment.

Genesis 49:29–32; 50:15–26a
Psalm 105
Matthew 10:24–33

Blessed be the God and Father of our Lord Jesus Christ, who has blessed us in Christ with every spiritual blessing in the heavens.

—EPHESIANS 1:3

The documentary film *Murderball* chronicles the lives of quadriplegic athletes who play for the Paralympic team competing for the gold medal in quad rugby. One young man deprived of all four limbs due to a rare childhood blood disorder spoke softly about what it takes to live with disability: "You use what you got, you maximize it." What use do we make of "every spiritual blessing in the heavens" available to us: wisdom, understanding, knowledge, counsel, courage, reverence, and wonder?

Amos 7:12–15
Psalm 85
Ephesians 1:3–14 or 1:3–10
Mark 6:7–13

We escaped with our lives
like a bird from the fowler's snare;
the snare was broken and we escaped.

—PSALM 124:7

Sometimes we suspect we're playacting at being faithful Christians. The rounds of religious practice are familiar and comforting, like entering the door of your childhood home. But times of crisis remind us just how serious faithful living is. Once, like the bird in the psalm, I barely escaped the fowler's snare with my life. I shuddered, wept, and placed my brokenness in the hands of God. The one who engineers our escape is the only one who can make us whole again.

Exodus 1:8–14, 22
Psalm 124
Matthew 10:34–11:1

Tuesday

JULY 14

• BD. KATERI TEKAKWITHA, VIRGIN •

*When the child grew, {his mother} brought him to Pharaoh's daughter,
who adopted him as her son and called him Moses; for she said, "I drew
him out of the water."*

—EXODUS 2:10

Surviving the vulnerability of childhood is the first hurdle
we cross. Moses, for instance, wasn't slaughtered with the
rest of his generation of male babies in Egypt. And Kateri
Tekakwitha, "the Lily of the Mohawks," did not succumb
to the smallpox that wiped out her family. But it did mark
her with a facial disfigurement for which she was deemed
unmarriageable. Yet this lily bloomed with inestimable
inner beauty that made her beloved. When she died,
witnesses say her body was transfigured by this loveliness.

Exodus 2:1–15a
Psalm 69
Matthew 11:20–24

⇒ 229 ⇐

Wednesday

JULY 15

• ST. BONAVENTURE, BISHOP AND DOCTOR OF THE CHURCH •

I give praise to you, Father, Lord of heaven and earth, for although you have hidden these things from the wise and the learned, you have revealed them to the childlike.

—MATTHEW 11:25

In his writings, Bonaventure shows us why he's called "the Seraphic Doctor" of the church to whom hidden things were revealed. He compares the soul's interior to the nine choirs of angels and their functions: "announcing, declaring, leading, ordering, strengthening, commanding, receiving, revealing, and anointing." The first three he identifies as human qualities. The next three are available only through effort. The final three are accessible only by grace. Which of these functions do you exercise best? Of which is the modern church most in need?

Exodus 3:1–6, 9–12
Psalm 103
Matthew 11:25–27

Thursday
JULY 16

• OUR LADY OF MOUNT CARMEL •

God replied {to Moses}, "I am who am."
—EXODUS 3:14

How do we know who God is and what God wants?
Carmelite Arnold Bostio wrote: "In the very vestibule of
memory, let {Mary} be the first . . . because she teaches
the ways of God." Catholics devoted to Mary need no
convincing. But for some, Marian devotion ranks just under
alien abduction on the list of inscrutable interests. Boomers
in particular were raised on traditional piety they often
reconsider critically. I wrote a book once for everyone
who's ever said to me, "What's up with Mary?" Key idea:
she never asked to be sealed in plaster.

Exodus 3:13–20
Psalm 105
Matthew 11:28–30

───────────

⇒ 231 ⇐

If you knew what this meant, "I desire mercy, not sacrifice," you would not have condemned these innocent men. For the Son of Man is Lord of the sabbath.

—MATTHEW 12:7–8

But Jesus (so my rebuttal goes), sacrifice is a far cleaner operation than mercy. Sacrifice is so definite—and happily finite. See how fast I can write out a check, or reach into my pocket for spare change. See how neatly I hand over that hour each weekend to go to church. Watch me graciously renounce all claims to the last Bavarian cream donut after Mass. Whereas mercy—as you know well, Lord—requires a change of heart. That gets complicated for messy hearts like mine.

Exodus 11:10–12:14
Psalm 116
Matthew 12:1–8

Behold, my servant whom I have chosen,
my beloved in whom I delight. . . .

—MATTHEW 12:18

A lot of sick children grow up to become doctors, nurses,
and therapists. Their early exposure to the healing
profession makes them naturals on the other side of the
stethoscope. Camillus de Lellis, after an early stint as
a soldier and gambler, wanted to join a religious order.
Chronic infirmities made him an unacceptable candidate.
So he started his own order, dedicated to the sick poor.
Those in need never argue that someone is unfit to
serve them.

Exodus 12:37–42
Psalm 136
Matthew 12:14–21

⇒ 233 ⇐

*But now in Christ Jesus you who once were far off have become near by
the blood of Christ.
For he is our peace. . . .*
—EPHESIANS 2:13–14

There was no way I was going to speak to the guy who
offended me again. *No way.* I repeated this mantra to fortify
my resolve. I was outraged. I was hurting. As I rehearsed,
for the twentieth time, the righteousness of my position
against my enemy, I remembered peace wasn't something
that was mine to give or to deny. Jesus is our peace. Jesus is
the *way* of peace. To withhold reconciliation is to withhold
Christ himself.

Jeremiah 23:1–6
Psalm 23
Ephesians 2:13–18
Mark 6:30–34

Monday

JULY 20

{The people} complained to Moses, . . . "Why did you do this to us?
Why did you bring us out of Egypt? . . . Far better for us to be the
slaves of the Egyptians than to die in the desert."

—EXODUS 14:11, 12

Slavery in Egypt or slain in the desert? The frying pan
or the fire? Plenty of us find ourselves at times facing two
equally unappealing alternatives. A therapist told me when
his clients present the two-pronged-destruction scenario,
he always advises them to choose "the third way." There
always is one, but it may require a bit of imagination to
see past the double doomsdays we've been staring into.
Neither slavery nor slaughter was what God had in mind
for Israel. Nor for us.

Exodus 14:5–18
Exodus 15:1bc–2, 3–4, 5–6
Matthew 12:38–42

I will sing to the LORD, for he is gloriously triumphant;
horse and chariot he has cast into the sea.

—EXODUS 15:1

A rabbi tells the story of God rebuking the angels at the Red Sea. They want to join in the victory canticle along with the Israelites as the water closes over the Egyptian chariots and charioteers. God silences them: "While my creatures are drowning in the sea you would sing a hymn?" This teaching reminds us that God does not rejoice in the death of the wicked. God's desire is always to save, never to destroy.

Exodus 14:21–15:1
Exodus 15:8–9, 10, 12, 17
Matthew 12:46–50

JULY 22

• ST. MARY MAGDALENE •

On the first day of the week, Mary of Magdala came to the tomb early in the morning, while it was still dark, and saw the stone removed from the tomb.

—JOHN 20:1

If ever a saint should sue for slander, Mary Magdalene has earned the right. Well-meaning Christians have called her a prostitute, while the New Age is abuzz about her alleged romance with Jesus. The Gospels say only that she suffered a terrible burden: "seven demons," the full complement of physical or mental infirmity. Jesus rescued her from the nightmare she was living and in return she surrendered her life to him. Her gratitude drove her fidelity all the way to the cross and the tomb.

Exodus 16:1–5, 9–15
Psalm 63
John 20:1–2, 11–18

But blessed are your eyes, because they see, and your ears, because they hear.

—MATTHEW 13:16

Visionaries are not beloved figures, neither in secular circles nor in the halls of established religion. The problem with those who have "the vision thing" is that they see things the rest of us don't—or won't. Bridget of Sweden's visionary writings are still hotly debated. "The world's riches are yours only for your necessary nourishment and clothing," she insisted. What does that say about my well-stocked pantry, my bursting closets, and my unnavigable garage?

Exodus 19:1–2, 9–11, 16–20b
Daniel 3:52, 53, 54, 55, 56
Matthew 13:10–17

Remember to keep holy the sabbath day. Six days you may labor and do all your work, but the seventh day is the sabbath of the LORD, your God.

—EXODUS 20:8–10

Which is the greatest commandment? When asked this question, Jesus offered the famous teaching about loving God and neighbor. But if you limited your choice to the Ten Commandments, chances are you wouldn't pick the one cited most often by the rabbis: the Sabbath imperative. It's not only one of the longest and most detailed of the commandments, but it's also the one that gets Jesus into the most trouble. Yet most of us labor seven days a week without thinking twice about Sabbath rest.

Exodus 20:1–17
Psalm 19
Matthew 13:18–23

Those who sow in tears
will reap with cries of joy.
Those who go forth weeping,
carrying sacks of seed,
Will return with cries of joy,
carrying their bundled sheaves.

—PSALM 126:5–6

One by one, the apostles, saints, and martyrs of the church
went out, bearing the sweet yoke of the gospel. One by
one, they faced rejection, persecution, and often death
for the love of Jesus. One by one, you and I march off
into history, claimed by our baptism and anointed by the
church for the exact same mission.

2 Corinthians 4:7–15
Psalm 126
Matthew 20:20–28

A man came . . . bringing . . . twenty barley loaves. . . . "Give it to the people to eat," Elisha said. But his servant objected, "How can I set this before a hundred men?"

—2 KINGS 4:42–43

The idea of *enough* continues to plague me. The need of the world is so great, and my resources are so puny. What good is my five dollars, or five hundred dollars, when whole communities are ravaged by disaster, disease, and war? What good is volunteering an hour with a child who needs a parent 24/7? What's one free meal when the person I feed will be hungry again tomorrow? Yet when each of us gives what we have, the miracle of multiplication occurs again.

2 Kings 4:42–44
Psalm 145
Ephesians 4:1–6
John 6:1–15

The kingdom of heaven is like yeast that a woman took and mixed with three measures of wheat flour until the whole batch was leavened.

—MATTHEW 13:33

Little things have great effects. A tablespoon of yeast is enough to make a bowlful of flour rise into fragrant and delicious bread. A word of praise elevates a heart. An invisible bit of DNA sets an innocent man free. So, too, a bad attitude ruins a party, a vicious rumor crushes a family, and a kindness withheld could mean the difference between life and death.

Exodus 32:15–24, 30–34
Psalm 106
Matthew 13:31–35

Then {Moses} said, "If I find favor with you, O LORD, do come along
in our company."
—EXODUS 34:9

What's the greatest thing that happens in the story of
Exodus? The ten plagues of Egypt looked awesome
in the movie. So did the dividing of the Red Sea. Of
course, Moses' face-to-face encounter with God is really
something. And the giving of the Ten Commandments is
nothing to sneeze at. But scholars say the most exciting
thing that happens in Exodus is that God agrees to keep
company with the people and to live in their midst. God-
with-us is still an exciting story.

Exodus 33:7–11; 34:5b–9, 28
Psalm 103
Matthew 13:36–43

Martha said to Jesus, "Lord, if you had been here, my brother would not have died. [But] even now I know that whatever you ask of God, God will give you."

—JOHN 11:21–22

Martha of Bethany would have given up everything for Jesus, I'm sure of it. She stood in the road with nothing left to lose after her brother Lazarus died. She violated the laws of decorum and told Jesus exactly what she thought: "Yes, Lord. I have come to believe that you are the Messiah, the Son of God, the one who is coming into the world" (John 11:27). Bold words—theologically outrageous and even blasphemous to some. Martha didn't care. The truth is always the most dangerous, and liberating, thing to say.

Exodus 34:29–35
Psalm 99
John 11:19–27 or Luke 10:38–42

Thursday

JULY 30

My heart and flesh cry out
for the living God.
—PSALM 84:3

Who will stand with those who cry out body and soul?
Among the newest saints in the church canon is Polish
Franciscan Simon of Lipnica. He cared for Krakow plague
victims in the fifteenth century until he died of plague
himself. He joins better-known saints like Damien the
Leper who shared the suffering of those whom he
served without reservation. Pope John Paul II named Simon
the patron of those who suffer from the poverty and
solitude imposed by injustice. St. Simon has his work cut
out for him.

Exodus 40:16–21, 34–38
Psalm 84
Matthew 13:47–53

Friday

JULY 31

• ST. IGNATIUS OF LOYOLA, PRIEST •

I, the LORD, am your God. . . .
—PSALM 81:11

Among the best-loved prayers of the church is the Suscipe
written by Ignatius of Loyola. Even if you can't say *soo-
she-pay* (Latin for "receive"), you know this prayer in some
form or another: "Take, Lord, and receive all my liberty,
my memory, my understanding, and my entire will, all I
have and call my own." It's a prayer for people ready to
surrender to God's goodness at last, who finally believe
that divine grace really is "enough for me."

Leviticus 23:1, 4–11, 15–16, 27, 34b–37
Psalm 81
Matthew 13:54–58

⇒ 246 ⇐

May God be gracious to us and bless us;
may God's face shine upon us.

—PSALM 67:2

In eighteenth-century Italy, the graciousness of God was by no means a given. Morality was taught with a heavy dose of fear and guilt. Then came Alphonsus Liguori, who believed that a sensitive and intelligent appeal to the heart was more attractive to the sinner in all of us. Named "Doctor of Morality and Marian Teaching," his sermons reflect a sympathetic understanding of the human condition: "All the days of their life, persons addicted to anger are unhappy, because they are always in a tempest." When in the tempest, Alphonsus is the one to call.

Leviticus 25:1, 8–17
Psalm 67
Matthew 14:1–12

{Y}ou should put away the old self of your former way of life . . . and put on the new self, created in God's way in righteousness and holiness of truth.

—EPHESIANS 4:22, 24

After what I considered a successful dinner party, my friend Dolores gave me the 411: "You dominated the conversation. You made the rest of us feel less interesting, less funny, less clever than you all night. Do you have to top every story?" I can't say which emotion was stronger in me: annoyance at being criticized, or mortification that Dolores might be onto something. What does one do with an unwelcome dollop of self-knowledge? Time to put away the old self, and try, try again.

Exodus 16:2–4, 12–15
Psalm 78
Ephesians 4:17, 20–24
John 6:24–35

[Jesus] said to them, "There is no need for {the crowds} to go away; give them some food yourselves."

—MATTHEW 14:16

The kingdom of God is not rocket science. It is, in fact, simple enough for a child to grasp. Is that woman hungry? Feed her. Is that man isolated? Welcome him. Is that family in danger? Offer them protection. Are those elderly folk homebound? Visit them. If we don't know what to do, it's not that we haven't been most carefully advised.

Numbers 11:4b–15
Psalm 81
Matthew 14:13–21

A clean heart create for me, God;
renew in me a steadfast spirit.

—PSALM 51:12

He was "just a parish priest," the man now known as the Curé d'Ars, and barely educated at that. Yet to those penitents who sought clean hearts, John Vianney spoke in terms easy to understand: "No, my dear brethren, even if you could perform miracles, you will never be saved if you have not charity. Not to have charity is not to know your religion; it is to have a religion of whim, mood, and inclination." Charity—*caritas*—love. The simple answer remains the best.

Numbers 12:1–13
Psalm 51
Matthew 14:22–36 or 15:1–2, 10–14

*Have pity on me, Lord, Son of David! My daughter is tormented
by a demon.*

—MATTHEW 15:22

You could tell by looking at the girl that she was troubled.
Something was eating at her, no doubt about it. But she
took great pains to hide it under a shaggy curtain of hair
and layers of clothes that obscured her body and weighted
her down like an albatross. The demon might be a family
secret, poor self-esteem, illness, or undiagnosed depression.
Her mother was determined to find a doctor, exorcist,
therapist, or *somebody* who could cast it out. Might Jesus be
the one?

Numbers 13:1–2, 25–14:1, 26a–29a, 34–35
Psalm 106
Matthew 15:21–28

And he was transfigured before them, and his clothes became dazzling white, such as no fuller on earth could bleach them. Then Elijah appeared to them along with Moses, and they were conversing with Jesus.

—MARK 9:2–4

Look who shows up at the transfiguration of Jesus—and who doesn't. Moses is the great teacher who enjoyed a unique intimacy with God. Elijah is the original wonder-working prophet. But David, the great king of Israel, is not in evidence; nor is Abraham, father of nations; nor Jacob, the original "Israel" himself. Jesus is not showcased according to a national or political role. He's a man of heaven, not of the world. His deeper identity is on display for those with eyes to see.

Daniel 7:9–10, 13–14
Psalm 97
2 Peter 1:16–19
Mark 9:2–10

Friday

AUGUST 7

• ST. SIXTUS II, POPE AND MARTYR, AND HIS COMPANIONS, MARTYRS •
ST. CAJETAN, PRIEST •

*What profit would there be for one to gain the whole world and forfeit
his life?*

—MATTHEW 16:26

What if the priest who baptized you had been defrocked?
Is the sacrament you received at his hands still valid?
Thank Pope Sixtus II for ruling that your spiritual life is
not forfeit, despite the status of the priest. Sixtus restored
relations with the heresy-riddled African Church by this
decree. It did not win him universal popularity: he was
dragged from his teaching chair and beheaded along with
some attendant deacons. But he confirmed that the grace
of the sacraments is gained for good.

Deuteronomy 4:32–40
Psalm 77
Matthew 16:24–28

———————————

{A} man {came up to Jesus}, knelt down before him, and said, "Lord, have pity on my son, for he is a lunatic and suffers severely; often he falls into fire, and often into water."

—MATTHEW 17:14–15

You don't have to be a lunatic to fall often into fire and into water. Or maybe it's a valid sign of lunacy if you do. Sometimes my heart burns for things that will not necessarily be good for me: a higher salary, greater prestige, or another helping of dessert. Just as often, I'm tepid about things that demand my strongest passion: prejudice, social injustice, and violence in faraway countries. Lord, have pity on me, and heal my heart's infirmity!

Deuteronomy 6:4–13
Psalm 18
Matthew 17:14–20

{Elijah} prayed for death: "This is enough, O LORD! Take my life, for I am no better than my fathers."

—1 KINGS 19:4

Is there a person alive who has never prayed for death like the prophet? In times of great want, life is a burden. When we are abandoned by love, death seems welcome. Humiliated or misunderstood, we would prefer to sink quietly into the earth rather than to go on breathing and feeling the anguish. Even Elijah, a worker of wonders and holy man of God, once prayed for death. God replied with food for the journey ahead. God continues to offer the same response to us.

1 Kings 19:4–8
Psalm 34
Ephesians 4:30–5:2
John 6:41–51

Monday

AUGUST 10

Consider this: whoever sows sparingly will also reap sparingly, and whoever sows bountifully will also reap bountifully.

—2 CORINTHIANS 9:6

I asked the holiest man I know: "How do I know when I've given enough?" He advised me: "Give until it scares you." Perhaps Deacon Lawrence used this formula when he gave away the whole treasury. Knowing the emperor's soldiers were on their way to seize the church's wealth, Lawrence emptied the parish coffers into the hands of the poor. Then, when demanded to produce the riches of the church, Lawrence gathered the poor from the streets, saying, "These are the treasures of the church."

2 Corinthians 9:6–10
Psalm 112
John 12:24–26

{The LORD} will be with you and will never fail you or forsake you. So do not fear or be dismayed.

—DEUTERONOMY 31:8

Clare of Assisi demonstrated complete confidence in God's faithfulness. It's tempting to say that she, like the dancer Ginger Rogers, did everything her famous collaborator did, only backwards and in high heels. But there was no competition between Francis and Clare in their jubilant race to the bottom. They shared a love for the riches only poverty could produce: utter reliance on God and the opportunity to encourage charity in their fellow citizens. Lovers of Lady Poverty are free of every possession but joy.

Deuteronomy 31:1–8
Deuteronomy 32:3–4ab, 7, 8, 9, 12
Matthew 18:1–5, 10, 12–14

⇒ 257 ⇐

Wednesday

AUGUST 12

• ST. JANE FRANCES DE CHANTAL, RELIGIOUS •

Come and see the works of God,
awesome in the deeds done for us.

—PSALM 66:5

Come and see marvelous works! A morning glory has
bloomed in my neighbor's yard, and is the only blue flower
on the street. The check arrived *before* the bills this month.
The smell of brewing coffee invites my rushed friend to
sit down. The child on the bicycle missed my shrubs this
time. Miracles happen all around us.

Deuteronomy 34:1–12
Psalm 66
Matthew 18:15–20

⇒ 258 ⇐

Peter {approached Jesus and} asked him, "Lord, if my brother sins
against me, how often must I forgive him?"

—MATTHEW 18:21

Are you with us or against us? When the sides are still
being drawn, the matter isn't always so certain. In the
early third century, Pontian was pope—and so was
Hippolytus, thereby making him technically an antipope.
The difference was lost on the Roman Emperor, who
sentenced both men to "the island of death" to work in
the mines. They died there of the harsh conditions, after
making peace with each other. The next pope buried them
together in the ultimate act of reconciliation.

Joshua 3:7–10a, 11, 13–17
Psalm 114
Matthew 18:21–19:1

Praise the LORD, who is so good;
God's love endures forever.
—PSALM 136:1

If you're not sure that God is love, or that God loves you in particular, it's hard to respond with love in return. Father Maximilian Kolbe was among the convinced. Trading his life for a family man chosen at random to die at Auschwitz, the priest displayed the same pastoral care he had always been remarkable for. At Kolbe's canonization forty years later, the man he had saved was present to testify that God's love endures forever in the graciousness of saints.

Joshua 24:1–13
Psalm 136
Matthew 19:3–12

While {Jesus} was speaking, a woman from the crowd called out and said to him, "Blessed is the womb that carried you and the breasts at which you nursed." He replied, "Rather, blessed are those who hear the word of God and observe it."

—LUKE 11:27–28

Her body was unique: in its depths the Word of God had been knit together with her own flesh and blood. But it was Mary's generous and lifelong "Yes!"—that one word—that made the Incarnate Word possible.

Vigil:	Day:
1 Chronicles 15:3–4, 15–16; 16:1–2	Revelation 11:19a; 12:1–6a, 10ab
Psalm 132	Psalm 45
1 Corinthians 15:54b–57	1 Corinthians 15:20–27
Luke 11:27–28	Luke 1:39–56

AUGUST 16

*"Come, eat of my food,
and drink of the wine I have mixed!
Forsake foolishness that you may live;
advance in the way of understanding."*

—PROVERBS 9:5–6

There are many ways to be foolish once we set our minds to it. But only one road to understanding presents itself, and that's found in response to the call of wisdom. As an attribute of God, wisdom has its source in divine truth. While knowledge can be gained in many learned fields— science, history, mathematics, literature—of themselves these cannot guarantee to make us wiser. Wisdom mediates mortal opportunity with moral responsibility, paving the road to the future in crystal clarity.

Proverbs 9:1–6
Psalm 34
Ephesians 5:15–20
John 6:51–58

{T}he Israelites offended the LORD by serving the Baals.
—JUDGES 2:11

The Baals still tempt us into their service. Take national
security, for example. In our desire to keep danger at bay,
we risk fostering a future of aggression, intimidation, and
prejudice against the evil *du jour*. Another modern Baal is
our standard of living. Even if global warming threatens
the planet, we're reluctant to downgrade our luxuries and
advantages. A final Baal is technology, which isolates us
as much as it claims to connect us. The Baals demand our
hearts. We can still say no.

Judges 2:11–19
Psalm 106
Matthew 19:16–22

Love and truth will meet;
justice and peace will kiss.
—PSALM 85:11

"All God wants is our heart." This observation by Jane
Frances de Chantal may seem like a common insight. Yet
many well-meaning folks in her day were convinced that
performing great acts of penance were more likely to win
God's favor. Even four centuries later, a lot of us
may suspect that religion is about hard work, rigorous
morality, and painful self-denial. The truth may be simpler
than we expect.

Judges 6:11–24a
Psalm 85
Matthew 19:23–30

Wednesday

AUGUST 19

• ST. JOHN EUDES, PRIEST •

"What if I wish to give this last one the same as you? [Or] am I not free to do as I wish with my own money? Are you envious because I am generous?" Thus, the last will be first, and the first will be last.

—MATTHEW 20:14–16

In worldly advantages, I am probably not first in line. But I'm certainly closer to the front of the line than the majority of people who ever lived on this planet. Which means, in kingdom terms, I should anticipate winding up close to the back of the line when the great reversal of justice takes place. Should I be worried? John Eudes supplies an escape clause: *humiliate in omnibus,* "humility in all things." Humility, the first of the virtues, is the practice of being last.

Judges 9:6–15
Psalm 21
Matthew 20:1–16

⇒ 265 ⇐

Thursday

AUGUST 20

• ST. BERNARD, ABBOT AND DOCTOR OF THE CHURCH •

To do your will is my delight;
my God, your law is in my heart!
—PSALM 40:9

Can the spiritual life be attractive in a world like ours?
Only if we, as individuals, become magnetic forces with
an irresistible example. Bernard of Clairvaux saved a
monastery from extinction by entering it—along with
thirty-one friends. By the time of his death, 700 monks had
joined him, and his order had expanded to 500 locations.
Named the "Devotional and Eloquent Doctor," Bernard
once said, "He who wears the easy yoke and light burden
of love will escape the intolerable weight of his own
self-will."

Judges 11:29–39a
Psalm 40
Matthew 22:1–14

⇒ 266 ⇐

*{F}or wherever you go I will go, wherever you lodge I will lodge, your
people shall be my people, and your God my God.*

—RUTH 1:16

These words of total devotion are familiar to anyone who's
ever been to a Catholic wedding. Yet the words are not
exchanged between lovers, as one might expect. Ruth
offers her undying fidelity here to Naomi, her *mother-in-law*.
This gives us pause because, in our culture, mothers-in-law
are most often the butt of jokes or the target of complaints.
Yet in the story of Ruth, the bond that exists between two
bereaved women is honored as among the noblest examples
of love in the Bible.

Ruth 1:1, 3–6, 14b–16, 22
Psalm 146
Matthew 22:34–40

"He will be your comfort and the support of your old age, for his mother is the daughter-in-law who loves you. She is worth more to you than seven sons!"

—RUTH 4:15

Why is Mary *Queen of Heaven?* Her coronation is not in the Bible. Her queenship was not formally a feast and teaching of the church until 1954. Yet the title first surfaced in the fourth century. Mary's royalty derives from the biblical image of Christ the King. If Jesus is the Prince of Peace of David's royal line, that makes Mary queen mother. Psychologist Carl Jung deemed this teaching brilliant, filling a human need to balance the patriarchy of heaven with a venerable female.

Ruth 2:1–3, 8–11; 4:13–17
Psalm 128
Matthew 23:1–12

AUGUST 23

Jesus then said to the Twelve, "Do you also want to leave?" Simon Peter answered him, "Master, to whom shall we go? You have the words of eternal life."

—JOHN 6:67–68

Crisis comes into every life. Jesus is no more a stranger to it than we are. After his most difficult teaching, many disciples give up on Jesus and go home. They were content to follow him when loaves and fishes were passed out, or when Jesus spoke against hated authorities and merciless laws. But when he pushed hard, the religious joyriders suspected the fun was over. Peter's words sound all the more brave and bold: *We're staying. Without you, there's no place to go.*

Joshua 24:1–2a, 15–17, 18b
Psalm 34
Ephesians 5:21–32 or 5:2a, 25–32
John 6:60–69

———

The wall of the city had twelve courses of stone as its foundation, on which were inscribed the twelve names of the twelve apostles of the Lamb.
—REVELATION 21:14

Some fishermen brothers in pairs. A political agitator. An empire-collaborating tax collector. A man known to be a thief. A loafer under a fig tree. The men who would become the twelve apostles were nothing special to start with. Jesus didn't choose them for their professional skills, their wisdom, or their personal piety. Yet these ordinary folks would be built into the eternal city of God as its foundation forever. One more reason not to say, "What possible use could God make of *me?*"

Revelation 21:9b–14
Psalm 145
John 1:45–51

> LORD, *you have probed me, you know me:*
> *you know when I sit and stand;*
> *you understand my thoughts from afar.*
> —PSALM 139:1–2

God is often described as omnipotent, omniscient, and omnipresent; that is, all-powerful, all-knowing, and everywhere. This used to be pretty intimidating information when we were kids. Was there no place we could hide, no thought we could harbor, without being intercepted by this Almighty invader? As we get older, the idea that nothing escapes the divine attention is increasingly comforting. I'd hate to have to be the one to keep track of world events for the celestial record.

1 Thessalonians 2:1–8
Psalm 139
Matthew 23:23–26

Woe to you, scribes and Pharisees, you hypocrites. You are like whitewashed tombs, which appear beautiful on the outside, but inside are full of dead men's bones and every kind of filth.

—MATTHEW 23:27

One of the hardest jobs we face is maintaining our integrity. We want our insides to match our outsides. But it's so much easier to simply polish the exterior person: speak honeyed words, put on fine clothes, dye the hair a more youthful color, and pretend to be something we're not. How much more difficult it is to change our hearts instead of our garments.

1 Thessalonians 2:9–13
Psalm 139
Matthew 23:27–32

Thursday

AUGUST 27

*What thanksgiving, then, can we render to God for you, for all the joy
we feel on your account before our God?*

—1 THESSALONIANS 3:9

It stands to reason that if we had more wives and mothers
like Monica out there, we'd see more children like St.
Augustine. Monica's Christian example was so attractive
and persuasive that it converted her pagan husband and,
eventually, even her morally tormented son. She lived
to see her son's baptism and died on the way home. All
parents who worry about their children's spiritual journeys
find a patron and friend in Monica.

1 Thessalonians 3:7–13
Psalm 90
Matthew 24:42–51

For God did not call us to impurity but to holiness.

—1 THESSALONIANS 4:7

Does religion take a dim view of money? Not according to the "Doctor of Grace," Augustine of Hippo: "Do you have wealth? It is a good thing. But only if your use of it is good. You will not be able to make good use of it if you are evil: wealth is an evil for the evil, a good for the good. Not that it is a good in the sense that it makes you good, but it is converted into good when it is in the hands of the good."

1 Thessalonians 4:1–8
Psalm 97
Matthew 25:1–13

{Herodias's daughter} went out and said to her mother, "What shall I ask for?" She replied, "The head of John the Baptist."
—MARK 6:24

All children crave the approval of their parents and will do anything to please them. But what if Mom is a spiteful woman with a thirst for blood? Herodias's desire for vengeance is so twisted that she willingly enlists her daughter's wish to serve. The result is the head of the Baptist served up on a platter. What could the girl do but hand it over to her mother? How did this ghastly event mark the person she would become?

1 Thessalonians 4:9–11
Psalm 98
Mark 6:17–29

AUGUST 30

Be doers of the word and not hearers only, deluding yourselves.
—JAMES 1:22

Jane handed me her much-coveted cookie recipe: "Now follow it exactly! I've got this down to a science." I set out immediately to duplicate her success. But the ingredients called for a shocking amount of sugar, so I cut it in half. And I substituted shortening for butter, and I always use whole wheat flour instead of white. The baking time seemed wrong, too, so I left them in longer. When the cookies came out of the oven, they were terrible! Something's wrong with that recipe.

Deuteronomy 4:1–2, 6–8
Psalm 15
James 1:17–18, 21b–22, 27
Mark 7:1–8, 14–15, 21–23

{The people of Nazareth} rose up, drove {Jesus} out of the town, and led him to the brow of the hill on which their town had been built, to hurl him down headlong. But he passed through the midst of them and went away.

—LUKE 4:29–30

The angry people swelled up like a bruise, acting in concert without brains or conscience. They pushed a single man forward, all the way out of town, to the edge of a cliff. In their outrage, no violence seemed unthinkable. Meanwhile, Jesus, the lone victim of their murderous intent, passed through their midst in cool deliberation. How did he do it? Did he part the crowd like Moses at the Red Sea? The will of a free person is stronger than the emotions of a mob.

1 Thessalonians 4:13–18
Psalm 96
Luke 4:16–30

Tuesday

SEPTEMBER 1

For all of you are children of the light and children of the day.
— 1 THESSALONIANS 5:5

As I watch, three young girls dash across a wooden bridge
that leads to the pavilion floating in the center of the lake.
Their hair streams behind them as their laughter echoes
across the water. They are the picture of childhood joy
and freedom as I remember it, dancing and whirling in
the pavilion as if nothing exists but this moment, this
happiness.

1 Thessalonians 5:1–6, 9–11
Psalm 27
Luke 4:31–37

Simon's mother-in-law was afflicted with a severe fever, and they interceded with {Jesus} about her. He stood over her, rebuked the fever, and it left her. She got up immediately and waited on them.

—LUKE 4:38–39

Once healed, the grateful woman responds with loving service. I have also been healed much, forgiven much, loved much. When will my service begin?

Colossians 1:1–8
Psalm 52
Luke 4:38–44

SEPTEMBER 3

After {Jesus} had finished speaking, he said to Simon, "Put out into deep water and lower your nets for a catch."

—LUKE 5:4

How deep are you willing to go for the great catch? Gregory the Great wrote: "There is nothing safer for defense than sincerity, nothing easier to say than truth. For, when obliged to defend its deceit, the heart is wearied with hard labor." I tested this theory when a friend rattled off the list of injuries he had suffered at my hands. And as he talked, I mentally prepared my rebuttal point for point in fierce denial. But when he completed the litany of my offenses, I decided to go deeper. "I'm sorry," I said. He hugged me!

Colossians 1:9–14
Psalm 98
Luke 5:1–11

Enter the temple gates with praise,
its courts with thanksgiving.
Give thanks to God, bless his name. . . .
—PSALM 100:4

It's been so long since I've counted my blessings. I hardly
know where to begin. My health, my home, my friends,
my job? All of these, certainly, must make the list. But let
me start small, with a slip of paper on my desk. It's colored
with a brown crayon, and HERSHEY'S ALMONDS is printed on
it in pencil. My niece made it for me when I said I wanted
a candy bar. Thank you, God, for so great a love as this.

Colossians 1:15–20
Psalm 100
Luke 5:33–39

Saturday

SEPTEMBER 5

O God, by your name save me.
By your strength defend my cause.
—PSALM 54:3

We all carry a special cause with us into prayer. The welfare of a loved one may be in jeopardy. Someone we know is sick or sad or burdened or lost. A lady at my church offers the same intercession every Sunday: "For my grandchildren—who are screwing up their lives!" We hear the pain of a grandmother watching yet another generation make the choices that will not lead to happiness. God has a special cause too: the grandmother, the kids, you, me, all of us.

Colossians 1:21–23
Psalm 54
Luke 6:1–5

{Jesus} said to him, "Ephphatha!"—(that is, "Be opened!") And [immediately] the man's ears were opened, his speech impediment was removed, and he spoke plainly.

—MARK 7:34–35

Eric regarded his father as a cipher. The man had sat mutely in front of the television set for forty years while Eric's mother had supplied his end of the conversation. Later in life, his father became ill and entered a nursing home. There he became alert and talkative, and had preferences and opinions never before given voice. Eric discovered that his father was a clever fellow with an engaging sense of humor. Without someone to speak for him, he had quite a lot to say.

Isaiah 35:4–7a
Psalm 146
James 2:1–5
Mark 7:31–37

Now I rejoice in my sufferings for your sake, and in my flesh I am filling up what is lacking in the afflictions of Christ on behalf of his body, which is the church. . . .

—COLOSSIANS 1:24

Is suffering useful? Are bodily aches or emotional deprivations in some way salvific? Many of us were told, when experiencing minor injury or injustice, to "offer it up" for a cause—the conversion of Russia or the souls in purgatory were both popular. It's difficult to imagine that heaven has a thriving economy reliant on pain as currency.

On the other hand, Paul argues the value of suffering based on the cross of Christ. Translating pain into spiritual rescue is better than throwing it away.

Colossians 1:24–2:3
Psalm 62
Luke 6:6–11

SEPTEMBER 8

• THE NATIVITY OF THE BLESSED VIRGIN MARY •

We know that all things work for good for those who love God, who are called according to his purpose.

—ROMANS 8:28

Birthdays are at least as important in the Bible as they are for us today. The church makes the birth of Jesus one of the greatest feasts of the year. The nativities of Mary and John the Baptist are also included on the church calendar. But don't forget the wonderful stories that surround the births of Moses, Samuel, and other biblical heroes. At every birth—including yours and mine—another player in salvation history is called into service.

Micah 5:1–4a or Romans 8:28–30
Psalm 13
Matthew 1:1–16, 18–23 or 1:18–23

—

⇒ 285 ⇐

Here there is not Greek and Jew, circumcision and uncircumcision,
barbarian, Scythian, slave, free; but Christ is all and in all.

—COLOSSIANS 3:11

Did applications for apostleship close at twelve? St. Paul described himself as the "Apostle to the Gentiles." Mary Magdalene has been called the "Apostle of Easter." The unnamed Samaritan woman at the well is known as the "Apostle of Samaria." Jesuit Peter Claver was called the "Apostle of the Negroes." He preferred the term "slave of the negroes forever," since he dedicated his life to championing and serving a people in chains. If God sends us on a mission, we too are apostles.

Colossians 3:1–11
Psalm 145
Luke 6:20–26

But to you who hear I say, love your enemies, do good to those who hate you, bless those who curse you, pray for those who mistreat you.
—LUKE 6:27–28

Tomorrow is another anniversary of 9/11. It may be hard for some to take these words of Jesus to heart at such a time. Yet Jesus says these words are only for those who hear him, those who have already opened their ears to his life-transforming message. The only way out of the global spiral of violence is to choose a way other than violence. Hating and destroying enemies only creates more hostility to go around.

Colossians 3:12–17
Psalm 150
Luke 6:27–38

SEPTEMBER 11

*I was once a blasphemer and a persecutor and an arrogant man,
but I have been mercifully treated because I acted out of ignorance in
my unbelief.*

—1 TIMOTHY 1:13

Might the world still learn a lesson from Paul of Tarsus?
His religious beliefs once compelled him to attack those
whom he sincerely believed were the enemies of God.
He was willing and even anxious to see them put to
death and pursued their destruction with zeal and single-
minded passion. He thought Christians were abhorrent
blasphemers and deserved to die. Then in a flash of
light, he lost his arrogance. His passion was fatefully
transfigured.

1 Timothy 1:1–2, 12–14
Psalm 16
Luke 6:39–42

*This saying is trustworthy and deserves full acceptance: Christ Jesus
came into the world to save sinners. Of these I am the foremost.*

—1 TIMOTHY 1:15

Humility didn't come easily to a man like Paul. He had
been convinced of the righteousness of his position against
Christianity, and he was dead wrong. Once he accepted
that, he understood the essential truth of Christ that
escapes many Christians. Jesus doesn't hate sinners. He
loves them. He doesn't want to destroy them, but gave his
life to save them. If we follow Jesus, we must not destroy
our enemies, but love them into new life.

1 Timothy 1:15–17
Psalm 113
Luke 6:43–49

SEPTEMBER 13

Along the way {Jesus} asked his disciples, "Who do people say that I am?"

—MARK 8:27

As you meet me along the way, dear Jesus, I give you many answers to your simple question. Sometimes I say you are the Lord of my religion, the one who commands, teaches, and compels me. At other times I say you are a sort of cosmic consolation prize for all the things that hurt humanity. You have been a friend, a companion, a truth sayer, and a rescuer. But only when I recognize you as Lord of my life can you make use of me.

Isaiah 50:5–9a
Psalm 116
James 2:14–18
Mark 8:27–35

{Jesus} emptied himself,
taking the form of a slave,
coming in human likeness;
and found human in appearance,
he humbled himself,
becoming obedient to death,
even death on a cross.

—PHILIPPIANS 2:7–8

In the inscrutable paradox of the reign of God, what goes down must come up. This applies if you're poor, meek, sick, sorrowful, persecuted, enslaved, despised, or in any way excluded. The exaltation of the cross is the first of many such astounding reversals.

Numbers 21:4b–9
Psalm 78
Philippians 2:6–11
John 3:13–17

*Behold, this child is destined for the fall and rise of many in Israel, and
to be a sign that will be contradicted (and you yourself a sword will
pierce) so that the thoughts of many hearts may be revealed.*

—LUKE 2:34–35

Most parents have felt this sword pierce their hearts. To
watch your child suffer is worse than suffering yourself.
If only you could remove every barrier to happiness in
your child's path! I knew a woman who actually attempted
to raise her daughter this way. In adulthood, the young
woman still lived in a world of pillows, dolls, and fantasy.
Her fear of hurt was so huge that she couldn't make friends
or take risks. Her loneliness was among the greatest hurts
I've seen.

1 Timothy 3:1–13
Psalm 101
John 19:25–27 or Luke 2:33–35

• ST. CORNELIUS, POPE AND MARTYR •
ST. CYPRIAN, BISHOP AND MARTYR •

*{Y}ou should know how to behave in the household of God, which is
the church of the living God, the pillar and foundation of truth.*

—1 TIMOTHY 3:15

It's fun, not to mention instructive, to note who shares
a feast on the church calendar. In the third century,
Pope Cornelius was reviled for being lenient with lapsed
Christians who had betrayed their faith during the
persecutions. After all, many had given their lives for this
creed! So why let these traitors back into the church?
Meanwhile, Cyprian, a friend to Cornelius, slammed
the door of rebaptism on schismatics. Both died in the
persecutions themselves, and may still be arguing their
differences in heaven.

1 Timothy 3:14–16
Psalm 111
Luke 7:31–35

SEPTEMBER 17

• ST. ROBERT BELLARMINE, BISHOP AND DOCTOR OF THE CHURCH •

Attend to yourself and to your teaching; persevere in both tasks, for by doing so you will save both yourself and those who listen to you.
—1 TIMOTHY 4:16

If you're tempted to think the road to canonization is paved with yes-men, consider Robert Bellarmine. He was trained as a Jesuit to teach *controversial theology*—of which the sixteenth century was full, thanks to the Reformation. His writings on papal power in secular affairs were questionable enough to almost merit listing on the index of forbidden books. Bellarmine was also a Galileo sympathizer. The cause for his canonization stalled for 300 years. Then he was named "Doctor of Church-State Relations." It may have been his first miracle!

1 Timothy 4:12–16
Psalm 111
Luke 7:36–50

Accompanying {Jesus} were the Twelve and some women who had been cured of evil spirits and infirmities, Mary, called Magdalene, from whom seven demons had gone out, Joanna, the wife of Herod's steward Chuza, Susanna, and many others who provided for them out of their resources.

—LUKE 8:1–3

Were the "evil spirits and infirmities" of the first century so different from ours? The seven demons of Mary Magdalene implied total infirmity: seven was shorthand for *fullness*. We don't much about what ailed her, or Joanna of Herod's household, or the mysterious Susanna. What we do know is that Jesus healed them all, and in their gratitude they could imagine no future that did not include his love and their service.

1 Timothy 6:2c–12
Psalm 49
Luke 8:1–3

Saturday

SEPTEMBER 19

• ST. JANUARIUS, BISHOP AND MARTYR •

*Knowledge of the mysteries of the kingdom of God has been granted
to you; but to the rest, they are made known through parables so that
"they may look but not see, and hear but not understand."*

—LUKE 8:10

If you're looking for mysteries, the Catholic Church is
full of them. Take Januarius, whose blood, preserved in
vials in Naples, has regularly liquefied since his death
in the fourteenth century. This qualifies him as one of
the incorruptibles: those saints whose bodies have been
preserved from the natural consequences of death. These
inexplicable signs remind us that death has no claim on
those who believe. Januarius is the patron saint of blood
banks and their donors. Today's a good day to make
a donation.

1 Timothy 6:13–16
Psalm 100
Luke 8:4–15

Where do the wars and where do the conflicts among you come from? Is it not from your passions that make war within your members?

—JAMES 4:1

What's the biggest source of conflict in your life? While it's tempting to point the finger at another person—a spouse, child, boss, or neighbor—chances are the finger should be pointing the other way. I know in my heart that it's *my* brooding, *my* lack of attention to my own needs, *my* judgmentalism, or *my* selfishness that's usually the culprit when I'm out of sorts. If I'm honest, I can normally tell what's wrong *and* how to fix it—without implicating another living soul.

Wisdom 2:12, 17–20
Psalm 54
James 3:16–4:3
Mark 9:30–37

And {Christ} gave some as apostles, others as prophets, others as evangelists, others as pastors and teachers, to equip the holy ones for the work of ministry, for building up the body of Christ. . . .
—EPHESIANS 4:11–12

When I was little, it seemed to me that apostles and prophets were the A-list of holiness. Regular saints were the second string, and priests and religious sisters followed soon after that. Then came the rest of us: slow and lumbering workhorses of the faith who are just getting the job done, one family and one decision at a time. Today I doubt there's a cosmic pyramid that looks like this. And I am more convinced that being a workhorse is by no means a fate without honor.

Ephesians 4:1–7, 11–13
Psalm 19
Matthew 9:9–13

SEPTEMBER 22

{Jesus} said to them in reply, "My mother and my brothers are those
who hear the word of God and act on it."

—LUKE 8:21

I saw the mother of Jesus today! In the middle of a dinner
party, she unabashedly took up a collection for the janitor
who had been pink-slipped earlier that day. I saw Jesus'
brothers and sisters, too. They considered the man's family,
reached into their pockets, and together amassed a sum
generous enough to keep the family afloat until a new
position could be secured.

Ezra 6:7–8, 12b, 14–20
Psalm 122
Luke 8:19–21

{I}n our servitude our God has not abandoned us. . . .
—EZRA 9:9

In our suffering we are not abandoned. Christ suffers
with us. The imprint of divine solidarity is visible in the
stigmatics—those upon whom the wounds of Christ have
been visited. Padre Pio is the best-known case in recent
times. The Catholic Encyclopedia Web site documents 321
stigmatics since Francis of Assisi. Some bear the stigmata
visibly; others suffer without apparent marks. Some bear a
single wound, as Margaret Mary Alacoque bore markings
like a crown of thorns. Each is a reminder that God suffers
until human suffering is ended.

Ezra 9:5–9
Tobit 13:2, 3–4a, 4befghn, 7–8
Luke 9:1–6

SEPTEMBER 24

But Herod said, "John I beheaded. Who then is this about whom I hear such things?"
—LUKE 9:9

Once the reign of God is in motion, you can't stop it. From the time of John the Baptist until now, the stage of history has been littered with martyrs. Every generation adds to the pile until our church calendar sags under the sheer weight of its martyrology. No matter how many messengers are murdered, the message continues to be told. You and I are only the latest participants to take up the Good News and share it far and wide.

Haggai 1:1–8
Psalm 149
Luke 9:7–9

Grant me justice, God;
defend me from a faithless people;
from the deceitful and unjust rescue me.

—PSALM 43:1

Fight my fight, Lord. Because you know what happens
when I fight it! Someone gets a bloody nose, or a tongue-
lashing from which they may not soon recover. When I try
to defend myself, even in a just cause, Lord, I often wind
up doing more harm than good and spreading the
ill will farther. My temper flares, my pride swells, and I
don't take prisoners. Only you know how to win the
victory for justice without creating a bigger mess than you
started with.

Haggai 2:1–9
Psalm 43
Luke 9:18–22

⇒ 302 ⇐

I will turn their mourning into joy,
I will console and gladden them after their sorrows.

—JEREMIAH 31:13

I wish the church might foster a special devotion to Cosmas and Damian today. Their example needs to be celebrated—and emulated. You've heard of Doctors Without Borders? These men were doctors without bills. As physicians of the second century, they became known as the "silverless ones" for practicing their healing craft without charge. Ask these saints to intercede for pro bono workers in every profession.

Zechariah 2:5–9, 14–15a
Jeremiah 31:10, 11–12ab, 13
Luke 9:43b–45

SEPTEMBER 27

{Eldad and Medad} too had been on the list, but had not gone out to the tent; yet the spirit came to rest on them also, and they prophesied in the camp.

—NUMBERS 11:26

What do we do when the *wrong* people are bearing the *right* message? Even heretics have had some wonderful things to say from time to time along with their errors. Pagan teachers like Aristotle and Plato were capable of brilliance. Martin Luther was right about some things, as even the church has since conceded. John Wesley wrote hymns now sung in Catholic liturgies. Even if some folks missed the meeting, it doesn't mean they weren't on the list of the Spirit's gifts.

Numbers 11:25–29
Psalm 19
James 5:1–6
Mark 9:38–43, 45, 47–48

Monday

SEPTEMBER 28

• ST. LAWRENCE RUIZ AND HIS COMPANIONS, MARTYRS •
ST. WENCESLAUS, MARTYR •

An argument arose among the disciples about which of them was the greatest.

—LUKE 9:46

Greatness begins in the heart. We see it active in the story of "Good King Wenceslas." As the familiar carol recounts, "on the feast of Stephen"—December 26th—the king sees a man gathering fuel on a bitter night. Wenceslas resolves to bring him home to dine. With his page in tow, the monarch heads out into the snow. The page protests against the cold, so the king invites the boy to follow in his footsteps, literally, to make the going easier. In our charity, we always walk behind the saints.

Zechariah 8:1–8
Psalm 102
Luke 9:46–50

Tuesday

SEPTEMBER 29

• ST. MICHAEL, ST. GABRIEL, AND ST. RAPHAEL, ARCHANGELS •

{B}efore the gods to you I sing.
—PSALM 138:1

As a guest visitor in a parochial school, I was suddenly asked to assume control of the fourth-grade religion class. What could I talk about that might possibly interest them? "Anybody here believe in angels?" I asked. The room came alive, with hands waving and children straining in their seats to be called on. We had a lively hour of fact sharing and personal testimonies. Kids are much more closely connected to the mystical dimension of things than the rest of us.

Daniel 7:9–10, 13–14 or Revelation 12:7–12a
Psalm 138
John 1:47–51

If I forget you, Jerusalem,
may my right hand wither.
—PSALM 137:5

By the fourth century, Christianity and Judaism were separate worlds. Those whose Lord had been killed under the charge, "the King of the Jews," were now bitterly estranged from their roots. Even the Bible, originally written in Hebrew and in Greek, was read exclusively in Latin. So Jerome taught himself Hebrew in order to return to the ancient texts and translate them freshly for the church. He was among the first to understand that Christians and Jews can never be far apart.

Nehemiah 2:1–8
Psalm 137
Luke 9:57–62

Thursday

OCTOBER 1

• ST. THÉRÈSE OF THE CHILD JESUS, VIRGIN AND DOCTOR OF THE CHURCH •

The decree of the LORD is trustworthy,
giving wisdom to the simple.
—PSALM 19:8

Thérèse, the third and most recent woman to be named a doctor of the church, bears the title "Doctor of Confidence and Missionaries." Her absolute trust in the benevolence of God made her seem, to some, cheeky and lacking in the proper humility. "My whole strength lies in prayer and sacrifice," she wrote. "These are my invincible arms; they can move hearts far better than words, I know it from experience." If we had Thérèse's confidence, perhaps we would pray as boldly as she did.

Nehemiah 8:1–4a, 5–6, 7b–12
Psalm 19
Luke 10:1–12

Friday

OCTOBER 2

See that you do not despise one of these little ones, for I say to you that their angels in heaven always look upon the face of my heavenly Father.
—MATTHEW 18:10

My favorite source for all things angelic is Vinita Hampton Wright's book, *A Catalogue of Angels: The Heavenly, the Fallen, and the Holy Ones Among Us.* Vinita has this to say about guardian angels: "Each person is guarded by an angel. Jerome stated: 'Great is the dignity of souls, for each one to have an angel deputed to guard it from its birth. . . .' Angels guard people in order to 'regulate them and move them to good.' The guardian never forsakes the person." For which we give thanks!

Baruch 1:15–22
Psalm 79
Matthew 18:1–5, 10

———————

OCTOBER 3

*I give you praise, Father, Lord of heaven and earth, for although you
have hidden these things from the wise and the learned you have revealed
them to the childlike.*

—LUKE 10:21

After giving a parish talk, I was surrounded by the usual
crowd of those who want to ask a question or offer a
rebuttal. From parish to parish, the concerns of this group
can be remarkably similar. Then a mother rescued me.
"My son wants to see you," she said. I followed her to the
eight-year-old. With great sincerity, the boy said, "I'm
sorry about your sister." My mouth dropped open. I had
mentioned my sister's death in the talk. This child alone
had offered condolences.

Baruch 4:5–12, 27–29
Psalm 69
Luke 10:17–24

Sunday

OCTOBER 4

*That is why a man leaves his father and mother and clings to his wife,
and the two of them become one body.*

—GENESIS 2:24

Francis de Sales had this to say about marriage: "If two
pieces of wood are carefully glued together, their union
will be so close that it is easier to break them in some fresh
place than where they were joined; and God so unites man
and wife, that it is easier to sever soul and body than those
two." I don't have to take Francis's word for it. Many of my
married friends say the same thing about their spouses.

Genesis 2:18–24
Psalm 128
Hebrews 2:9–11
Mark 10:2–16

OCTOBER 5

*But the LORD sent a large fish, that swallowed Jonah; and he remained
in the belly of the fish three days and three nights.*

—JONAH 2:1

It's no wonder that the episode of a prophet being
swallowed by a fish became earmarked as "the sign of
Jonah." Whatever else happened to Jonah wouldn't top
that! The sign of Jonah was later considered an Old
Testament type (think *archetype*) of the time Jesus spent in
the tomb before Easter morning. We also use this sign to
speak of the experience of loss itself—how its darkness
swallows us whole. Jonah's release is a good sign for all
of us.

Jonah 1:1–2:2, 11
Jonah 2:2, 3, 4, 5, 8
Luke 10:25–37

Martha, Martha, you are anxious and worried about many things.
There is need of only one thing. Mary has chosen the better part and it
will not be taken from her.

—LUKE 10:41–42

Marthas and Marys of the world, unite! You may well end
up sharing a feast day together. Marie-Rose Durocher,
definitely a "Martha" type, founded a congregation of
teaching sisters in Canada and set up schools for poor
young women. Bruno, scandalized by the life of his bishop
at the cathedral in Rheims, founded the Carthusian order
and spent the rest of his life between hermitages and
monasteries. He was a natural "Mary." Praise God we've
got plenty of both kinds to serve the church.

Jonah 3:1–10
Psalm 130
Luke 10:38–42

{Jesus} was praying in a certain place, and when he had finished, one of his disciples said to him, "Lord, teach us to pray just as John taught his disciples."

—LUKE 11:1

My younger sister once prayed the rosary in an hour of adolescent desperation. She wanted to see the latest *Star Wars* movie but no one had materialized to offer her a ride to the theater. Just in time, a friend called: she'd snared her mother's car! My sister was never sure if the Blessed Mother supplied the car or not. But she decided that those beads were powerful stuff. The next time she lifted a rosary, she'd find a nobler cause.

Jonah 4:1–11
Psalm 86
Luke 11:1–4

OCTOBER 8

They are like a tree
planted near streams of water,
that yields its fruit in season;
Its leaves never wither;
whatever they do prospers.

—PSALM 1:3

Mystics see connections the rest of us might miss. So the psalmist saw the relationship between trees and human faithfulness. Thirteenth-century German mystic Mechtild of Magdeburg saw human life as a grand waltz with the divine. "I cannot dance, O Lord, unless you lead me," she wrote. This is prayer enough for any day.

Malachi 3:13–20b
Psalm 1
Luke 11:5–13

OCTOBER 9

• ST. DENIS, BISHOP AND MARTYR, AND COMPANIONS, MARTYRS •
ST. JOHN LEONARDI, PRIEST •

Whoever is not with me is against me,
and whoever does not gather with me scatters.

—LUKE 11:23

Seven bishops were sent to convert the citizens of Gaul in
the third century. They were put to death in Paris. Today,
Denis, one of those bishops, is the patron saint of France.
Why do we so often kill our heroes first and honor them
later? Saints are easier to deal with when they're dead and
gone. But their challenging example remains to haunt us.

Joel 1:13–15; 2:1–2
Psalm 9
Luke 11:15–26

Saturday

OCTOBER 10

Crowd upon crowd
in the valley of decision;
For near is the day of the LORD
in the valley of decision.

—JOEL 4:14

Our faith is not proven in the hour of prayer. Nor do
we show ourselves to be true disciples of Jesus when we
partake of sacraments. It's in the valley of decision, that
anxious and confusing place, where we demonstrate who
we are and what we really believe.

Joel 4:12–21
Psalm 97
Luke 11:27–28

OCTOBER 11

Indeed, the word of God is living and effective, sharper than any two-edged sword, penetrating even between soul and spirit, joints and marrow, and able to discern reflections and thoughts of the heart.

—HEBREWS 4:12

God's word is alive, the writer of Hebrews tells us. It's not just an inert group of letters on a page, but a message that penetrates us body and spirit. This reminds us of another saying, from the first chapter of John's Gospel: "And the Word became flesh / and made his dwelling among us" (14). The same word once incarnate in Jesus is now alive and well and expressing itself through us.

Wisdom 7:7–11
Psalm 90
Hebrews 4:12–13
Mark 10:17–30 or 10:17–27

Through {Christ Jesus} we have received the grace of apostleship, to bring about the obedience of faith, for the sake of his name, among all the Gentiles, among whom are you also, who are called to belong to Jesus Christ. . . .

—ROMANS 1:5–6

I was baptized on Columbus Day some fifty years ago. In my childhood imagination, the exciting journey to the New World and my entry into the life of the church somehow got warped together. Of course, our faith *is* a journey that takes us to places sometimes wondrous and sometimes perilous. The grace of apostleship, as St. Paul calls it, means we are first and foremost *sent*. If we stay just as we are, we miss the adventure.

Romans 1:1–7
Psalm 98
Luke 11:29–32

———————

OCTOBER 13

The heavens declare the glory of God;
the sky proclaims its builder's craft.

—PSALM 19:2

Each day, sunrise is the first evidence of the existence
of God, as far as I can tell. Sunset is not quite the last,
because after that, we have a glittering heaven full of stars.
Maybe it helps to live in the Southwest, where there's a lot
more sky to consider. Out here, you'd have to work really
hard at being an atheist.

Romans 1:16–25
Psalm 19
Luke 11:37–41

⇒ 320 ⇐

Therefore, you are without excuse, every one of you who passes judgment. For by the standard by which you judge another you condemn yourself, since you, the judge, do the very same things.
—ROMANS 2:1

Can a former slave and embezzler become a pope? It happened in the third century. Callistus had been sent to the dreaded mines of Sardinia for bank fraud. A well-placed woman friend arranged his release. Later, after assuming the papacy, he was criticized for being too lenient with those who committed sexual misdemeanors. Maybe it's easier to forgive big sinners when you've been one yourself. Or maybe Callistus took Paul's words to the Romans to heart.

Romans 2:1–11
Psalm 62
Luke 11:42–46

Thursday

OCTOBER 15

• ST. TERESA OF JESUS, VIRGIN AND DOCTOR OF THE CHURCH •

What occasion is there then for boasting? It is ruled out. On what principle, that of works? No, rather on the principle of faith.

—ROMANS 3:27

I would have named her "Doctor of Common Sense." The church calls Teresa "Doctor of Prayer." She was awfully good at that, as Bernini's famous sculpture, *The Ecstasy of S. Teresa di Àvila*, deftly portrays. But she was also skilled at chess, dancing, and horseback riding. Teresa delighted in puncturing false piety with wit: "We are not angels but have bodies, and it is madness for us to want to become angels while we are still on earth, and as much on earth as I was."

Romans 3:21–30
Psalm 130
Luke 11:47–54

⇒ 322 ⇐

Friday

OCTOBER 16

• ST. HEDWIG, RELIGIOUS • ST. MARGARET MARY ALACOQUE, VIRGIN •

Be glad in the LORD and rejoice, you just;
exult, all you upright of heart.
—PSALM 32:11

The upright do not shrink from worldly matters, as
Hedwig of Silesia proves. A sort of thirteenth-century
Hillary Clinton, she married into politics at twelve, and the
union strengthened the position of husband King Henry
I. But later Hedwig herself became prominent in affairs
of state. Her courage and gentleness were legendary, and
with her husband she founded monasteries and houses of
religious women. Silesia, now divided between Poland and
the Czech Republic, has since vanished. The memory of
Hedwig outlasts her earthly kingdom.

Romans 4:1–8
Psalm 32
Luke 12:1–7

⩾ 323 ⩽

I tell you, everyone who acknowledges me before others the Son of Man will acknowledge before the angels of God.

—LUKE 12:8

The ink was barely dry on the texts that now make up our New Testament when Ignatius of Antioch wrote letters to his fellow saint, Polycarp. Ignatius is credited with the first recorded use of the word *catholic* to describe the church. He also wrote: "The very reason you are given a body as well as a soul is to help you gain the favor of this outward and visible world." How can I use my hands, my feet, my strength, and my words to acknowledge Christ before others?

Romans 4:13, 16–18
Psalm 105
Luke 12:8–12

OCTOBER 18

For we do not have a high priest who is unable to sympathize with our weaknesses, but one who has similarly been tested in every way, yet without sin.

—HEBREWS 4:15

In a 2001 poll cited by the *New Yorker,* more than half of American Catholics, Lutherans, Methodists, and Presbyterians believed that Jesus sinned—contrary to the doctrine their leaders teach. Back to square one: Jesus is *without sin.* The Bible says he was tempted, so he knows what we're up against. Paul writes in 2 Corinthians 5:21 about how Jesus was also made "to be sin" for us. This means Jesus accepted death, the "wage of sin," so that it would be paid once and for all.

Isaiah 53:10–11
Psalm 33
Hebrews 4:14–16
Mark 10:35–45 or 10:42–45

• ST. JOHN DE BRÉBEUF AND ST. ISAAC JOGUES, PRIESTS AND MARTYRS,
AND THEIR COMPANIONS, MARTYRS •

Then {Jesus} said to the crowd, "Take care to guard against all greed,
for though one may be rich, one's life does not consist of possessions."

—LUKE 12:15

Jesus is always busting our chops about money in Luke's
Gospel. It's enough to make a moderately successful
American wince. The truth is, Luke was writing precisely
for a well-to-do audience like ours. Luke's patron—a
person or group known only as *Theophilus*, "lover of God"—
had the kind of position in society only money could buy.
Luke tailored his message from the tradition he'd received
to make his Gospel as pertinent—and as challenging—as
possible for the community that had commissioned it.

Romans 4:20–25
Luke 1: 69–70, 71–72, 73–75
Luke 12:13–21

Where sin increased, grace overflowed all the more. . . .
—ROMANS 5:20

Here's the great mystery of sin and grace: the abundance of God's grace not only compensates for the channel dug by sin, but overwhelms its banks until what results is far better than anything that could have been before the sin. This is how we get the "wounded healer," from whose infirmity many find their cure. This is also why we find saints quite often in the conversion of notorious sinners. The darkest hour of your life could be the starting point of your salvation.

Romans 5:12, 15b, 17–19, 20b–21
Psalm 40
Luke 12:35–38

———————————

Had not the LORD been with us,
let Israel say,
Had not the LORD been with us,
when people rose against us,
They would have swallowed us alive,
for their fury blazed against us.

—PSALM 124:1–3

So many times, when the world seems poised against us, God finds us a path to safety. If it means opening a road through the sea, keeping us alive in the desert, or championing our lives against desperate odds, God is willing to make a miraculous effort to save us. When you feel overwhelmed by the forces mounting against you— familial, financial, medical, spiritual—trust in God's track record of salvation.

Romans 6:12–18
Psalm 124
Luke 12:39–48

For the wages of sin is death, but the gift of God is eternal life in Christ Jesus our Lord.

—ROMANS 6:23

In adolescence, some of us were attracted to the disorderly living that quickly becomes harmful, even deadly. We didn't sleep regularly or eat healthily. Perhaps we abused our bodies with drink, cigarettes, and other drugs. We may have been careless with our sexuality, or with our hearts and those of others. We were, in other words, young and foolish. Many of us wake up to the fatal cards we're playing in plenty of time to choose life. Those who don't keep racking up that deadly wage.

Romans 6:19–23
Psalm 1
Luke 12:49–53

When you see [a] cloud rising in the west you say immediately that it is going to rain—and so it does; and when you notice that the wind is blowing from the south you say that it is going to be hot—and so it is. You hypocrites! You know how to interpret the appearance of the earth and the sky; why do you not know how to interpret the present time?

—LUKE 12:54–56

In the wonderful movie *Groundhog Day*, Bill Murray is the ultimate swaggering meteorologist. He can tell you anything you want to know about the weather. But he is totally clueless about the realm of his own heart. He cannot predict where his present road is taking him or envision what tomorrow may bring. The only way to do that is to turn our gaze from what's out there and do a little survey of what's going on inside.

Romans 7:18–25a
Psalm 119
Luke 12:54–59

The concern of the flesh is death, but the concern of the spirit is life and peace.

—ROMANS 8:6

The average priest or deacon might wonder at the end of his life how many sermons he'd preached. The official score for Bishop Anthony Mary Claret is 25,000, which could be the record to beat. But sheer volume isn't what makes a preacher great. It's what you say. Anthony wrote in his autobiography, "Choose now what you would wish to have chosen at life's end." This could be the sermon of a lifetime.

Romans 8:1–11
Psalm 24
Luke 13:1–9

Jesus said to him in reply, "What do you want me to do for you?" The blind man replied to him, "Master, I want to see."

—MARK 10:51

How courageous Bartimaeus is, to yell out when he hears Jesus is passing! The crowd rebukes him, but he doesn't care. This is his big chance! When Jesus calls him, he drops the cloak in which he'd collected his livelihood of offerings. He's serious: he doesn't intend to go back to begging. In fact, he's the *only* man Jesus cures who becomes a disciple. But once you can see, isn't it obvious where your path lies?

Jeremiah 31:7–9
Psalm 126
Hebrews 5:1–6
Mark 10:46–52

This daughter of Abraham, whom Satan has bound for eighteen years now, ought she not to have been set free on the sabbath day from this bondage?

—LUKE 13:16

There are two responses we can make to the Sabbath day observance. One is that it's too holy a day to do any work. The other is that it's too holy a day to withhold any grace possible to bestow. The Pharisees cut the corners of the observance narrowly, and try to restrain any unessential task. The only argument Jesus has with that is that the health, wholeness, and happiness of an infirm woman *is* an essential matter in his book.

Romans 8:12–17
Psalm 68
Luke 13:10–17

OCTOBER 27

Again he said, "To what shall I compare the kingdom of God? It is like yeast that a woman took and mixed [in] with three measures of wheat flour until the whole batch of dough was leavened."

—LUKE 13:20–21

Every Gospel has its special themes. Luke is known for the prominence of women in his stories. Jesus brakes for females in need, whether they are old women or mere children. He even breaks the Sabbath for them! Jesus includes women among his followers, who are seen as the financial backers of his ministry. (See the start of chapter 8.) And here, Jesus compares God's reign to the activity of a woman. For women and those who love them, this is all good news.

Romans 8:18–25
Psalm 126
Luke 13:18–21

{Y}ou are no longer strangers and sojourners, but you are fellow citizens with the holy ones and members of the household of God, built upon the foundation of the apostles and prophets, with Christ Jesus himself as the capstone.

—EPHESIANS 2:19–20

Jude had no speaking parts in the Gospels, but he made up for it in the lore of popular devotion. Where would we go with our lost causes if we couldn't bring them to Jude? His image is as familiar to us as fellow apostle Simon's is obscure. Ever see a statue of Simon? I didn't think so. Yet he's the natural patron saint of political zealots. Whether you're passionate about the environment, universal health care, minority rights, or peace, Simon is your guy.

Ephesians 2:19–22
Psalm 19
Luke 6:12–16

OCTOBER 29

For I am convinced that neither death, nor life, nor angels, nor principalities, nor present things, nor future things, nor powers, nor height, nor depth, nor any other creature will be able to separate us from the love of God in Christ Jesus our Lord.

—ROMANS 8:38–39

Nothing means nothing when Paul says it. No possible barriers to God's love exist because Jesus has broken down every one, even death. No powers in heaven, no present or future action, no conceivable dimension can be imagined in which God's love is not available and operative. So why are we afraid? Why do we sometimes think that we have already forfeited God's love because of our stupidity? Stupidity is just one more "creature" brushed aside when God sets out to love us.

Romans 8:31b–39
Psalm 109
Luke 13:31–35

OCTOBER 30

Then {Jesus} said to them, "Who among you, if your son or ox falls into a cistern, would not immediately pull him out on the sabbath day?"

—LUKE 14:5

Sometimes it's the rules we are willing to break, and not the ones we follow, that define us.

Romans 9:1–5
Psalm 147
Luke 14:1–6

Happy those whom you guide, LORD,
whom you teach by your instruction.
You give them rest from evil days. . . .
—PSALM 94:12–13

Among the more mournful movements in fundamentalism today is the shunning of Halloween. What was once viewed as a delightful evening of make-believe, and a rare chance for the whole neighborhood to play together—kids and adults alike—has now become a battleground in the war between good and evil. We have so few opportunities to knock on a neighbor's door and say hello. Do it tonight, even if you're a very old kid! (Blackened teeth optional.)

Romans 11:1–2a, 11–12, 25–29
Psalm 94
Luke 14:1, 7–11

Beloved, we are God's children now; what we shall be has not yet been revealed. We do know that when it is revealed we shall be like him, for we shall see him as he is.

—1 JOHN 3:2

Look in the mirror. What you see is God's child. Not the one who once lay in a manger, but the one who was born to your mother and father in circumstances unique to you. Look into the future. What you will be is yet to be revealed. But one thing is for sure: a child of God remains a child of God.

Revelation 7:2–4, 9–14
Psalm 24
1 John 3:1–3
Matthew 5:1–12a

———————

For if before men, indeed, they be punished,
yet is their hope full of immortality;
Chastised a little, they shall be greatly blessed,
because God tried them
and found them worthy of himself.

—WISDOM 3:4–5

The end. Those two words used to be a fitting conclusion to any story. But only certain tales ended with the more encouraging finale: *And they all lived happily ever after.* But what if there were no end at all? What if happily ever after just went on and on? This is the promise Isaiah holds out for that day when death itself faces *the end.*

Wisdom 3:1–9
Psalm 103
Romans 5:5–11 or 6:3–9
John 6:37–40

NOVEMBER 3

• ST. MARTIN DE PORRES, RELIGIOUS • ELECTION DAY •

Rejoice in hope,
endure in affliction,
persevere in prayer.
—ROMANS 12:12

Back in 1962, Pope John XXIII canonized Martin de Porres
and named him the patron saint of interracial justice.
We needed such a saint in the civil rights' sixties, and
can hardly dispense with such a patron today. Martin,
of African and Spanish heritage, was a barber-surgeon
before joining the Dominicans as a lay brother. He became
renowned as a healer of both physical and spiritual
suffering. Our world still suffers the pain of racial division.
Martin is ready to intercede and to serve.

Romans 12:5–16
Psalm 131
Luke 14:15–24

Happy are those who fear the LORD,
who greatly delight in God's commands.
Their descendants shall be mighty in the land,
a generation upright and blessed.

—PSALM 112:1–2

November is the month for saints, those who "delight in God's commands." Some folks of an earlier generation grew weary of these plaster guardians staring from every corner of the average parish. Their children and grandchildren arrived into a church from which the saints have nearly vanished. To stem the tide, I've become a bit of a "saint lady." I've got statues in my yard and portraits on my walls. These are our heavenly relatives. I'm happy to hold the celestial family reunion at my house.

Romans 13:8–10
Psalm 112
Luke 14:25–33

NOVEMBER 5

For if we live, we live for the Lord,
and if we die, we die for the Lord;
so then, whether we live or die, we are the Lord's.

—ROMANS 14:8

When my friend Dale was diagnosed with brain cancer, we gathered with friends in his hospital room for the anointing of the sick. Sitting in a circle, we each prayed for a blessing from the Holy Spirit. One prayed for healing; another for hope. Dale himself prayed for courage. As a man of faith, he knew that life and death are in God's hands. The one thing he needed most was the fortitude to embrace his fate as it unfolded.

Romans 14:7–12
Psalm 27
Luke 15:1–10

*{T}he master commended that dishonest steward for acting prudently.
For the children of this world are more prudent in dealing with their own
generation than are the children of light.*

—LUKE 16:8

The dishonest steward in Jesus' most vexing parable is not
a good guy. First, he squanders his master's property and
gets called on the carpet for it. Then, while settling the
accounts before his dismissal, he cooks the books one more
time. Yet this unscrupulous fellow winds up the hero of
the story. Why? Because, like most selfish folks, he shows
absolute dedication to *number one*. Jesus would like to see
the same level of dedicated service from those of us who
claim Jesus as our *number one*.

Romans 15:14–21
Psalm 98
Luke 16:1–8

The person who is trustworthy in very small matters is also trustworthy in great ones; and the person who is dishonest in very small matters is also dishonest in great ones.

—LUKE 16:10

After leaving a stressful professional position, my friend Kim took a low-paying office job. The first day, her new boss asked her to do some filing. There was quite a stack; evidently the person she'd replaced had not made filing a priority. So Kim started alphabetizing and made a day of it. The very next morning, the boss gave her a substantial raise. For practicing her alphabet! She figured if Kim took such care with the files, she could trust her with anything.

Romans 16:3–9, 16, 22–27
Psalm 145
Luke 16:9–15

NOVEMBER 8

The LORD protects the stranger,
sustains the orphan and the widow,
but thwarts the way of the wicked.

—PSALM 146:9

Three kinds of people were continuously promised
protection and preservation in the Old Testament:
strangers, orphans, and widows. We still hold a soft spot
for the women and children, but strangers are currently
off the list of social concern. Ancient Israel was committed
to hospitality toward the aliens in their land, precisely
because they knew what it was like to be vulnerable
and without rights. Today many are convinced that
undocumented people deserve no welcome, assistance, or
kindness. God's protection is all they have.

1 Kings 17:10–16
Psalm 146
Hebrews 9:24–28
Mark 12:38–44

For we are God's co-workers; you are God's field, God's building.

—1 CORINTHIANS 3:9

Twice each year, we mark the feast day of a basilica. Is a building worth celebrating? Ask the folks who've just closed a deal on a new home, or rented a space for their own small business. Ask parishioners who will have Mass this weekend in the church for which they raised funds over the past ten years. Ask townspeople who have finally gotten their first fire station, health clinic, or recreation center. Many dreams for the future begin with a humble slab of cement.

Ezekiel 47:1–2, 8–9, 12
Psalm 46
1 Corinthians 3:9c–11, 16–17
John 2:13–22

Those who trust in {the Lord} shall understand truth,
and the faithful shall abide with him in love. . . .

—WISDOM 3:9

Few of us have enthusiasm for truth of the doctrinal sort. But it would be a mistake to consider Leo the Great, "Doctor of Doctrine," to be a person of purely philosophical concerns. He did fight the heretical teachings of his generation; but he also simultaneously defended Rome from Vandals and Huns—no theoretical matter! This dual defense seems a very wise course to imitate. We should guard against "doctrinal drain" as well as more aggressive assaults to our faith.

Wisdom 2:23–3:9
Psalm 34
Luke 17:7–10

Wednesday

NOVEMBER 11

• ST. MARTIN OF TOURS, BISHOP • VETERANS DAY •

Hear, therefore, kings, and understand;
learn, you magistrates of the earth's expanse! . . .
Because, though you were ministers of {God's} kingdom, you judged not
rightly,
and did not keep the law,
nor walk according to the will of God. . . .

—WISDOM 6:1, 4

Many a soldier comes back from war a confirmed pacifist.
In the third century, Martin of Tours, from a military
family, began his career in the tradition of his fathers. But
the injustice of the war in which he was required to fight
changed his mind about killing. He agreed to carry the
cross into battle, risking his life, but would not bear arms.
He may be the first recorded Christian pacifist. But he
would not be the last.

Wisdom 6:1–11
Psalm 82
Luke 17:11–19

For in {Wisdom} is a spirit
intelligent, holy, unique,
Manifold, subtle, agile,
clear, unstained, certain. . . .

—WISDOM 7:22

In the popular mind, people like Mohandas K. Gandhi and Martin Luther King Jr. may be saints. But the Roman Catholic Church rarely canonizes anyone outside of its membership. Bishop Josaphat was the first Eastern Rite Catholic to be formally recognized in the Roman canon. (It's noteworthy that he supported the union of the Ukrainian Church with Rome and was killed by opponents of the union.) The impulse remains a good one: to recognize holiness wherever we find it.

Wisdom 7:22b–8:1
Psalm 119
Luke 17:20–25

Friday

NOVEMBER 13

• ST. FRANCES XAVIER CABRINI, VIRGIN •

One day to the next conveys that message;
one night to the next imparts that knowledge.
—PSALM 19:3

Speaking about spiritual values is a small part of religious education. Mother Cabrini wanted the teachers in her schools to live those values in an environment of love, calling this "the education of the heart." Parents who are worried about how to raise their children in the church might tuck this phrase away. The education of the heart outlives every other lesson we might learn or teach.

Wisdom 13:1–9
Psalm 19
Luke 17:26–37

NOVEMBER 14

But when the Son of Man comes, will he find faith on earth?

—LUKE 18:8

Jesus was not in the habit of asking rhetorical questions. Each of us must decide personally if we will live the faith Jesus is looking for.

Wisdom 18:14–16; 19:6–9
Psalm 105
Luke 18:1–8

But of that day or hour, no one knows, neither the angels in heaven, nor the Son, but only the Father.

—MARK 13:32

We don't know the hour that this world will pass away, or, for that matter, how it will happen. More personally, we don't even know which precise breath will be our last one. What we *are* clear on is that the clock is ticking, and that there's no time to lose. If we're going to clean up our act, today's the day.

Daniel 12:1–3
Psalm 16
Hebrews 10:11–14, 18
Mark 13:24–32

⇒ 353 ⇐

They told him, "Jesus of Nazareth is passing by."
—LUKE 18:37

Awareness of the presence of Jesus is a hallmark of
sainthood. But saints known as "great" seem to have a
special gift for embodying Jesus for others. Popes, kings,
and theologians have been called "great," but Gertrude
is the only female to earn the title. She was a thirteenth-
century German nun and mystic. After examining the
inadequacies of her life, Gertrude came to this humble
resolve: "I know what I will do . . . I will place Jesus'
chalice on the empty scales of Truth. Thus, I will make
amends for everything I lack." That sounds like a plan with
greatness in it.

1 Maccabees 1:10–15, 41–43, 54–57, 62–63
Psalm 119
Luke 18:35–43

Tuesday

NOVEMBER 17

• ST. ELIZABETH OF HUNGARY, RELIGIOUS •

This is how {Eleazar} died, leaving in his death a model of courage and an unforgettable example of virtue not only for the young but for the whole nation.

—2 MACCABEES 6:31

Elizabeth of Hungary died of exhaustion—a kind of martyrdom rarely acclaimed. She was a princess exiled from court after her husband's death by relatives who feared her charity would drain the royal coffers. Elizabeth sold her remaining jewelry and clothes to build a hospital, and lived the remainder of her life as a tertiary Franciscan caring for the poor. Miracles were attributed to her in her lifetime. But the greatest miracle is that she, born to wealth, slipped through the needle's eye with ease.

2 Maccabees 6:18–31
Psalm 3
Luke 19:1–10

• THE DEDICATION OF THE BASILICAS OF ST. PETER AND ST. PAUL, APOSTLES • ST. ROSE-PHILIPPINE DUCHESNE, VIRGIN •

{The king replied}, "Well done, good servant! You have been faithful in this very small matter; take charge of ten cities."

—LUKE 19:17

Sometimes, for reasons known only to God, we don't get our heart's desire. French-born Sr. Rose Duchesne had always longed to work with the people of the New World, but didn't make it to the Potawatomi mission until she was too old and frail to be of much practical use. Still, the Potawatomi called her "the woman who prays always" for her long hours in fervent prayer. As we all discover, when you are where God wants you to be, you're always on time.

2 Maccabees 7:1, 20–31
Psalm 17
Luke 19:11–28
or (for the memorial of the dedication):
Acts 28: 11–16, 30–31
Psalm 98
Matthew 14:22–33

---

*As {Jesus} drew near {Jerusalem}, he saw the city and wept over it,
saying, "If this day you only knew what makes for peace—but now it
is hidden from your eyes."*

—LUKE 19:41–42

How many cities does Jesus weep over today? How many
nations cause his compassionate heart to break for all the
missed opportunities to know God's *shalom*?

1 Maccabees 2:15–29
Psalm 50
Luke 19:41–44

For all in heaven and on earth is yours;
yours, O LORD, is the sovereignty;
you are exalted as head over all.
—1 CHRONICLES 29:11

When we speak of God as *sovereign*, we're saying God's in charge. Acknowledging God's sovereignty means accepting that it's God's world and that divine authority is bigger than all the powers of earth. But even after we throw crowns, governments, and worldly authorities in the dust before God, we have to remember to add the one vital power that most often sets itself in opposition to God: our own stubborn will.

1 Maccabees 4:36–37, 52–59
1 Chronicles 29:10bcd, 11abc, 11d–12a, 12bcd
Luke 19:45–48

I will praise you, LORD, with all my heart;
I will declare all your wondrous deeds.

—PSALM 9:2

According to legend, Mary was presented at age twelve to serve the temple. There, she praised God by weaving cloth for ritual use. On the Sabbath day, she spoke only with the angels. In some Renaissance paintings of this scene, the angels form a virtual halo around her. Hebrew religion did not utilize female virgins in their temple as the pagans did, so these events are likely unhistorical. But the idea of little Mary in conversation with angels reminds us that one such conversation would soon change the world.

1 Maccabees 6:1–13
Psalm 9
Luke 20:27–40

So Pilate said to {Jesus}, "Then you are a king?"
—JOHN 18:37

Lord Jesus, even Pilate was willing to grant you a kingship in the end. He nailed his confession as well as your crime to the cross: "Jesus the Nazorean, the King of the Jews" (19:19). When the religious leaders objected, Pilate refused to recant what he had written. But writing the truth, even believing it, isn't the same as living it. Lord, give us the courage to live what we profess.

Daniel 7:13–14
Psalm 93
Revelation 1:5–8
John 18:33b–37

• ST. CLEMENT I, POPE AND MARTYR • ST. COLUMBAN, ABBOT •
BD. MIGUEL AGUSTÍN PRO, PRIEST AND MARTYR •

Blessed are you on the throne of your kingdom,
praiseworthy and exalted above all forever.

—DANIEL 3:54

Often we take religious freedom for granted. But in the
early twentieth century, religious practices were banned by
the revolutionary government of Mexico. Miguel Agustín
Pro had to flee his country before finishing seminary and
was ordained abroad. Returning to Mexico, he resorted
to disguises and took refuge in safe houses where he
administered sacraments and taught catechetics. His final
words before the firing squad were, "Viva Cristo Rey!"
(Long live Christ the King!) Pray for all who still await the
day of religious liberty.

Daniel 1:1–6, 8–20
Daniel 3:52, 53, 54, 55, 56
Luke 21:1–4

Tuesday

NOVEMBER 24

• ST. ANDREW DUNG-LAC, PRIEST AND MARTYR, AND HIS COMPANIONS, MARTYRS •

{T}he God of heaven will set up a kingdom that shall never be destroyed or delivered up to another people; rather, it shall break in pieces all these kingdoms and put an end to them, and it shall stand forever.

—DANIEL 2:44

For many of us, going to church is a weekly decision. But it's hardly a life-or-death situation. How hard it is to imagine the history of the church in Vietnam: four centuries bloodied by persecutions. Thousands, including Fr. Andrew Dung-Lac and his companions, were tortured and murdered. Tens of thousands lost their homes and their lands for their faith. Each Sunday, we debate whether to put a five or a ten in the basket. What if our very lives were required of us?

Daniel 2:31–45
Daniel 3:57, 58, 59, 60, 61
Luke 21:5–11

⇒ 362 ⇐

Wednesday

NOVEMBER 25

• ST. CATHERINE OF ALEXANDRIA, VIRGIN AND MARTYR •

Remember, you are not to prepare your defense beforehand, for I myself shall give you a wisdom in speaking that all your adversaries will be powerless to resist or refute.

—LUKE 21:14–15

Ever been taunted by those who do not share your faith? If such occasions find you maddeningly tongue-tied, try asking for the intercession of Catherine of Alexandria. She had the intellectual stamina to challenge the emperor himself about idol worship. He responded by sending fifty philosophers to talk her down. They failed; in fact, she converted all of them instead. Our goal is not to know what Catherine knew, but to believe as she believed.

Daniel 5:1–6, 13–14, 16–17, 23–28
Daniel 3
Luke 21:12–19

⋛ 363 ⋚

Let the earth bless the Lord,
praise and exalt him above all forever.
—DANIEL 3:74

Rendering thanks by eating our brains out sounds like an odd proposition. But you won't get any complaints from me. Bring on the turkey, stuffing, yams, and cranberry sauce, and don't forget the pumpkin pie! More importantly, invite someone who might otherwise be alone to the table to share the feast. And give generously so that others will have a reason this day to give thanks.

Daniel 6:12–28
Daniel 3:68, 69, 70, 71, 72, 73, 74
Luke 21:20–28

Heaven and earth will pass away, but my words will not pass away.
—LUKE 21:33

Lyrics from love songs. Snippets of dialogue from movies.
Jingles from television commercials. Heavens, the things
that get lodged in our minds! Why not make a genuine
effort to memorize a few words that have staying power
for eternity? Each week write down one verse of Scripture,
post it on your bathroom mirror, and commit it to memory.
In a year, you've got a treasure chest of living words to
enrich your life.

Daniel 7:2–14
Daniel 3:75, 76, 77, 78, 79, 80, 81
Luke 21:29–33

NOVEMBER 28

*I, Daniel, found my spirit anguished within its sheath of flesh, and I
was terrified by the visions of my mind.*

—DANIEL 7:15

Do nightmares of apocalyptic horror frighten you? There's
nothing in the books of Daniel, Ezekiel, or Revelation—or
in the Gospels or the writings of Paul for that matter—that
should keep you awake at night. Wherever we find images
of cataclysmic destruction in the Bible, they are always
followed with assurances that God will rescue the just
from all harm and from every evil. What *should* cause us
every concern is, frankly, whether or not you and I can be
counted among the just.

Daniel 7:15–27
Daniel 3: 82, 83, 84, 85, 86, 87
Luke 21:34–36

The liturgical calendar does not count years from January 1 to December 31, but rather from the first Sunday of Advent through the last Saturday of ordinary time. The church year has just ended. Tomorrow begins a new cycle of readings that will continue through November 27, 2010.

If these daily thoughts have blessed you this year, now is the time to get 2010: *A Book of Grace-Filled Days*, by Alice Camille. The readings that follow are taken from that book, so you can switch from 2009 to 2010 anytime this month. Pick it up or order it from your local bookstore, or order it online at www.loyolabooks.org.

*The days are coming, says the LORD, when I will fulfill the promise I
made to the house of Israel and Judah.*

—JEREMIAH 33:14

Promises are among the loveliest things on the earth.
Lovers delight in the vows they speak to each other.
Children thrive on the promises of their parents. Our
sacraments are each tangible covenants between God and
us. The only thing better than a promise is its fulfillment.
That's why every Advent journey ends in Bethlehem.

Jeremiah 33:14–16
Psalm 25
1 Thessalonians 3:12–4:2
Luke 21:25–28, 34–36

Their voice has gone forth to all the earth,
and their words to the ends of the world.

—ROMANS 10:18

Was Andrew the first disciple to follow Jesus? John's
Gospel says Andrew started out as a follower of John the
Baptist and then switched allegiances when his own teacher
pointed to "the Lamb of God." Andrew then went looking
for his brother Peter to tell him the Good News. This was
a fateful recruitment in the life of the church to come.
Andrew's story reminds us to "each one, bring one." If the
news is really good, it's worth sharing.

Romans 10:9–18
Psalm 19
Matthew 4:18–22

Then the wolf shall be a guest of the lamb,
and the leopard shall lie down with the kid;
The calf and the young lion shall browse together,
with a little child to guide them.
The cow and the bear shall be neighbors,
together their young shall rest;
the lion shall eat hay like the ox.
The baby shall play by the cobra's den,
and the child lay his hand on the adder's lair.

—ISAIAH 11:6–8

Nature has resolved her differences and fear is a thing of the past in Isaiah's lovely vision. Can there ever be such a world? Only when the earth is "filled with knowledge of the Lord" (verse 9), says the prophet. How do we begin this journey of understanding?

Isaiah 11:1–10
Psalm 72
Luke 10:21–24

My heart is moved with pity for the crowd, for they have been with me now for three days and have nothing to eat. I do not want to send them away hungry, for fear they may collapse on the way.

—MATTHEW 15:32

Jesus looks out on a hungry world and feels compassion. He resolves to feed all future generations on his own life.

Isaiah 25:6–10a
Psalm 23
Matthew 15:29–37

Thursday

DECEMBER 3

• ST. FRANCIS XAVIER, PRIEST •

*"Open up the gates
to let in a nation that is just,
one that keeps faith.
A nation of firm purpose you keep in peace;
in peace, for its trust in you."*
—ISAIAH 26:2–3

Some religious leaders rule by fear, using rigid rules or images of harsh punishments in the hereafter to keep people in line. Francis Xavier had other ideas, which he urged on his fellow missionaries: "Labor with all your might to gain for yourselves the love of the people. You will be far better able to help them if they love you than if they fear you." Those who win our love become our greatest teachers.

Isaiah 26:1–6
Psalm 118
Matthew 7:21, 24–27

Friday

DECEMBER 4

• ST. JOHN OF DAMASCUS, PRIEST AND DOCTOR OF THE CHURCH •

On that day the deaf shall hear
the words of a book;
And out of gloom and darkness,
the eyes of the blind shall see.
—ISAIAH 29:18

Is your secret ambition to be a doctor of the church? If
so, here's some advice: write a book! Church doctors are
chosen not for their powers of healing but for their facility
at teaching the faith. John of Damascus, the "Doctor of
Images," earned his title not from making images but by
protecting them. He insisted that saints' likenesses are
important because these men and women "have kept intact
that image of God in which they were created." Do others
see God's likeness in us?

Isaiah 29:17–24
Psalm 27
Matthew 9:27–31

Then {Jesus} said to his disciples, "The harvest is abundant but the laborers are few; so ask the master of the harvest to send out laborers for his harvest."

—MATTHEW 9:37–38

Don't just pray for vocations this year. Embrace one! This is our annual invitation to come work in the vineyard of the Lord. God calls all of us to something. It's our responsibility to discern what that call means for us. Take your vocation seriously: go on retreat, get spiritual direction, talk to wise and holy people, think about it. If you're married, pray together and seek discernment as a couple or as a family. The abundant harvest needs you!

Isaiah 30:19–21, 23–26
Psalm 147
Matthew 9:35–10:1, 5a, 6–8

For God has commanded
that every lofty mountain be made low,
And that the age-old depths and gorges
be filled to level ground,
that Israel may advance secure in the glory of God.

—BARUCH 5:7

We know this familiar prophecy from Isaiah: Every valley will be exalted, and every hill be brought low. The prophet Baruch gives the well-known ending a twist. These massive landscape alterations are not done simply to "prepare the way of the Lord" (Isaiah 40:3). They are also to prepare a level route *for us* to advance to God. What mountains need to come down, what gorges filled in, so that you can move forward in holiness this Advent?

Baruch 5:1–9
Psalm 126
Philippians 1:4–6, 8–11
Luke 3:1–6

DECEMBER 7

• ST. AMBROSE, BISHOP AND DOCTOR OF THE CHURCH •

Love and truth will meet;
justice and peace will kiss.
—PSALM 85:11

The happy embrace of virtues in the psalm is something
we'd all like to enjoy. But it doesn't happen by magic.
Ambrose became the "Pastoral Doctor" by teaching others
how to acquire virtue's embrace. For this he became so
beloved that he was elected bishop by popular demand,
even before he was baptized! Ambrose wrote, "The first
exercise in training the soul is to turn away sin, the second
to implant virtue." It's not enough to stop behaving badly.
We have to replace ornery behavior with good behavior.

Isaiah 35:1–10
Psalm 85
Luke 5:17–26

⇒ 376 ⇐

DECEMBER 8

• THE IMMACULATE CONCEPTION OF THE BLESSED VIRGIN MARY •

I will put enmity between you and the woman,
and between your offspring and hers;
He will strike at your head,
while you strike at his heel.

—GENESIS 3:15

Dogma can be hard to appreciate even with some book learning. In an earlier era, when education was rare, art was the most popular teaching tool of the church. To appreciate this, check out images of the Immaculate Conception. Artists portray Mary standing on a globe and crushing a serpent underfoot. This image echoes the story of original sin entering the world through the poisonous designs of the serpent. The dastardly plan was thwarted by the one woman who could trample sin with impunity.

Genesis 3:9–15, 20
Psalm 98
Ephesians 1:3–6, 11–12
Luke 1:26–38

Take my yoke upon you and learn from me, for I am meek and humble of heart; and you will find rest for yourselves.

—MATTHEW 11:29

"Meek and humble of heart" describes Juan Diego, a poor Indian of Mexico who came to Christianity at the age of fifty. Our Lady appeared to him three times and blessed him with roses in winter and an indelible image of herself on his cloak. She also consoled Juan, an elderly widower without children: "Am I not here, who is your Mother? Are you not under my protection?" No one who seeks this protection will be left unaided.

Isaiah 40:25–31
Psalm 103
Matthew 11:28–30

DECEMBER 10

The afflicted and the needy seek water in vain,
their tongues are parched with thirst.
I, the LORD, will answer them;
I, the God of Israel, will not forsake them.
—ISAIAH 41:17

How long, O Lord, how long? So many are afflicted, and so many are needy. My prayer list grows heavy with cancers and depressions, troubled marriages and chemical addictions, unemployment and ravaging loneliness. Most days, it seems everybody I know is thirsty. You alone can satisfy them, which is why I make my prayer to you.

Isaiah 41:13–20
Psalm 145
Matthew 11:11–15

DECEMBER 11

• ST. DAMASUS I, POPE •

Happy those who do not follow
the counsel of the wicked . . .
Rather, the law of the LORD is their joy;
God's law they study day and night.

—PSALM 1:1, 2

Here's a feast day for the Bible-study crowd, as well as
for those who are middling faithful to their page-a-day
reflections. Committing ourselves to daily contact with
Scripture—even the tiny verse at the top of the page—is
the spiritual equivalent of taking a multivitamin. Thank
Pope Damasus for that. He commissioned the great biblical
scholar Jerome to make a new and faithful translation of
the Bible available to the church. Where would we be
without the good word?

Isaiah 48:17–19
Psalm 1
Matthew 11:16–19

A great sign appeared in the sky, a woman clothed with the sun, with the moon under her feet, and on her head a crown of twelve stars.

—REVELATION 12:1

Next to the European Madonnas of my youth, Our Lady of Guadalupe seems astonishingly attired. Her robes are often portrayed in bright scarlet and green, instead of the pale Marian blues I'd grown used to. Her blazing full-body halo seems electrifying next to the thin gold circlet she otherwise demurely wears on her head. It's as if Mary went to Mexico and went native! Which is precisely the point of her apparition there. Mary our mother *is* native to every land, and every people.

Zechariah 2:14–17 or Revelation 11:19a; 12:1–6a, 10ab
Psalm 45
Luke 1:26–38 or 1:39–47

*I am baptizing you with water, but one mightier than I is coming.
. . . His winnowing fan is in his hand to clear his threshing floor and
to gather the wheat into his barn, but the chaff he will burn with
unquenchable fire.*

—LUKE 3:16, 17

John the Baptist predicted that the wheat would be
gathered and saved, and the chaff would be cast out and
burned. No wonder he was confused when, in prison, he
heard that Jesus was gathering the chaff of society *and
forgiving them*, and casting out the righteous as unprepared
and undeserving! Did John get it wrong? Or have we
simply misunderstood the categories?

Zephaniah 3:14–18a
Isaiah 12:2–3, 4bcd, 5–6
Philippians 4:4–7
Luke 3:10–18

Make known to me your ways, LORD;
teach me your paths.
Guide me in your truth and teach me,
for you are God my savior.
—PSALM 25:4–5

Kidnapped, imprisoned, beaten, and starved—bad treatment under any circumstances. But John of the Cross endured these things at the hands of fellow Carmelites! Thinking differently in community life can be costly. Later, this mystical doctor would write *Dark Night of the Soul* to illuminate the path of spiritual desolation. Bitterness would be only human, given his experience. But John preferred another response. He wrote: "The only language {God} hears is the silent language of love."

Numbers 24:2–7, 15–17a
Psalm 25
Matthew 21:23–27

DECEMBER 15

Jesus said to them, "Amen, I say to you, tax collectors and prostitutes are entering the kingdom of God before you."

—MATTHEW 21:31

We can imagine throngs lined up ahead of us as we await our own spiritual evaluation on the last day. There are so many in front of us, all bearing the dispositions, opinions, and professions of people we have judged and condemned. What if God doesn't see them as we do—doesn't reject them outright as clearly undeserving? What if God offers them the same blanket amnesty we are hoping to obtain for ourselves?

Zephaniah 3:1–2, 9–13
Psalm 34
Matthew 21:28–32

DECEMBER 16

Let justice descend, O heavens, like dew from above,
like gentle rain let the skies drop it down.

—ISAIAH 45:8

Tonight, the Advent novena of *Posadas*, or "Lodgings,"
begins. Many in our Latino community will go door-to-
door as Joseph and Mary once did, seeking hospitality
from friends and parishioners. The first two times they will
be denied entrance, but in the end there will be welcoming,
praying, and feasting. We can all participate in the spirit of
Posadas by making sure that hospitality is a virtue regularly
exercised toward family, friends, and strangers alike—
especially the disadvantaged in our midst.

Isaiah 45:6b–8, 18, 21b–25
Psalm 85
Luke 7:18b–23

DECEMBER 17

Jacob called his sons and said to them: "Assemble and listen, sons of Jacob, listen to Israel, your father."

—GENESIS 49:1–2

Our parents' blessing is a powerful thing. Bestowed, or withheld, it has a wide-ranging effect on our lives. When Jacob blesses his sons, he gives them what they need, not necessarily what they deserve. Judah was not the first-born, not a strong leader, and certainly not Jacob's favorite. But he is given the authority to rule and a place in the genealogy that will spool out all the way to Bethlehem. Never hold onto a blessing when you can set it free to act in history!

Genesis 49:2, 8–10
Psalm 72
Matthew 1:1–17

"Behold, the virgin shall be with child and bear a son,
and they shall name him Emmanuel,"
which means "God is with us."
—MATTHEW 1:23

One week before Christmas, and as usual I'm far from
ready. My house is a wreck, the shopping's not done,
there's nights of baking and wrapping ahead, and
Christmas cards will have to wait until the New Year—
again. But I still have seven days to do the one thing
needful: get my heart in order to receive the child of
dreams. If nothing else is ready, Lord Jesus, make me ready.

Jeremiah 23:5–8
Psalm 72
Matthew 1:18–25

For the boy shall be consecrated to God from the womb, until the day of his death.

—JUDGES 13:7

Lots of children in the Bible were mysteriously announced, consecrated, and employed by God before they were born. Take Abraham's brood, foretold to be as numerous as the stars when the old man and Sarah were still childless. Consider Samson in today's reading from Judges, who would become the Hebrew "Superman." Or Samuel: the future prophet, priest, and judge. Don't forget Elizabeth's son, and Mary's. Is it possible you and I were likewise decreed? That we are on a mission we only dimly suspect?

Judges 13:2–7, 24–25a
Psalm 71
Luke 1:5–25

Sunday
DECEMBER 20

• FOURTH SUNDAY OF ADVENT •

Blessed are you who believed that what was spoken to you by the Lord would be fulfilled.

—LUKE 1:45

The pregnant women come together; one is much older and more obviously advanced in her condition than the other. They contain a mystery the rest of us don't quite appreciate. They know that new life starts inside, unfolds from the first *yes*. They know this brave new life requires ongoing commitment, care, time, and the grace of God. They know they can't do it without God, nor does God choose to do it without them. They know they are God's partners in bringing hope to birth.

Micah 5:1–4a
Psalm 80
Hebrews 10:5–10
Luke 1:39–45

⇒ 389 ⇐

My lover speaks; he says to me,
"Arise, my beloved, my beautiful one,
and come!"

—SONG OF SONGS 2:10

"By charity's beautiful engagements" we are bound to each other. I think I know what Peter Canisius meant when he used this wonderful phrase. When I meet others who love what I love and seek what I seek—when I find companions who are sharing the spiritual journey—it's as if I've known them forever. We are, at once, joyfully joined at the heart. Such friendships do not leave us, even in death.

Song of Songs 2:8–14 or Zephaniah 3:14–18a
Psalm 33
Luke 1:39–45

DECEMBER 22

I prayed for this child, and the LORD granted my request. Now I, in turn, give him to the LORD; as long as he lives, he shall be dedicated to the LORD.

—1 SAMUEL 1:27–28

Mothers and fathers parade through the Bible. One by one, they surrender their children to God's purposes. Wise parents today do the same thing. They know they cannot possess these little people. They cannot keep them from all harm nor orchestrate their every decision. The best they can do is make an offering of these little lives to God. Even if your children are not so small, God's still listening.

1 Samuel 1:24–28
1 Samuel 2:1, 4–5, 6–7, 8abcd
Luke 1:46–56

{W}ho will endure the day of his coming?
And who can stand when he appears?

—MALACHI 3:2

Each child conceived is a child of destiny. If we believe in life as a sacred trust, then it would be perilous to consider any person undeserving of love, respect, food, water, shelter, medical assistance, education, and a chance to become the wonder God intended.

Malachi 3:1–4, 23–24
Psalm 25
Luke 1:57–66

DECEMBER 24

I have made a covenant with my chosen one;
I have sworn to David my servant:
I will make your dynasty stand forever
and establish your throne through all ages.

—PSALM 89:4–5

Jesus comes into our world at the darkest time of the year,
on the shortest day, when hope seems farthest from us.
Jesus promises to be with us always in the darkest hour,
"Lo, to the end of time!"

2 Samuel 7:1–5, 8b–12,14a, 16
Psalm 89
Luke 1:67–79

For a child is born to us, a son is given us;
upon his shoulder dominion rests.
They name him Wonder-Counselor, God-Hero,
Father-Forever, Prince of Peace.

—ISAIAH 9:5

They will name this child other things, too. He is Justice-
Champion, Rescuer of Sinners, No-More-Fear, Honor
for the Shamed, Mourner's Joy, Touch of Healing,
Homecoming for Outcasts, Hope of the Desperate, and
the Empty Tomb. For now, he's only a baby. Just wait.

Vigil
Isaiah 62:1–5
Psalm 89
Acts 13:16–17, 22–25
Matthew 1:1–25 or 1:18–25
Midnight
Isaiah 9:1–6
Psalm 96
Titus 2:11–14
Luke 2:1–14
Dawn
Isaiah 62:11–12
Psalm 97
Titus 3:4–7
Luke 2:15–20
Day
Isaiah 52:7–10
Psalm 98
Hebrews 1:1–6
John 1:1–18 or 1:1–5, 9–14

DECEMBER 26

• ST. STEPHEN, FIRST MARTYR •

Into your hands I commend my spirit;
you will redeem me, LORD, faithful God.
—PSALM 31:6

We knew it was Dale's last Christmas. We asked what
he wanted for the holiday meal. "Goose!" he shouted.
So a friend cooked the goose—easier said than done.
We served the ancient bottle of Russian wine saved for a
special occasion. We ate too much, drank a lot, talked and
laughed, and told sparkling, wonderful stories. The day
after Christmas, Dale passed into unconsciousness. He left
us the stories, still winking with vitality even today.

Acts 6:8–10; 7:54–59
Psalm 31
Matthew 10:17–22

{Jesus} went down with them and came to Nazareth, and was obedient to them; and his mother kept all these things in her heart.

—LUKE 2:51

Many mothers and fathers know quite well what Mary kept in her treasure-chest heart: the terror of losing sight of your child, even for a moment. The anxiety of watching your child take risks. The pain of watching your child hurt. The yearning to see your child attain lasting happiness. All parents have treasure-chest hearts. Holy families understand that sometimes obedience requires great sacrifice.

Sirach 3:2–6, 12–14 or 1 Samuel 1:20–22, 24–28
Psalm 128
Colossians 3:12–21 or 3:12–17 or 1 John 3:1–2, 21–24
Luke 2:41–52

{T}he angel of the Lord appeared to Joseph in a dream and said, "Rise, take the child and his mother, flee to Egypt, and stay there until I tell you. Herod is going to search for the child to destroy him."

—MATTHEW 2:13

The dark spirit of Herod still wanders the world, in search of children to destroy. Some will perish in the womb, others by frailty or disease, accident or abuse. Some will grow up a little, only to face the dangers of drugs and alcohol, fast cars and ill-chosen friends. St. Joseph, guardian of children, gather all of our lost, needy, and endangered sons and daughters into your special protection.

1 John 1:5–2:2
Psalm 124
Matthew 2:13–18

DECEMBER 29

This is the way we may know we are in union with {Jesus}: whoever
claims to abide in him ought to live [just] as he lived.

—1 JOHN 2:5–6

A CEO was recently quoted as saying, "The person who
takes one step ahead of others is a leader. The person
who takes three steps ahead is a martyr." Thomas Becket
was many steps ahead of his king when he refused to
allow the church to be used as a pawn of the state. Those
called to leadership in families, parishes, workplaces, and
government often find themselves needing to take that
next prophetic step. Pray for leaders until it's your turn to
exercise leadership.

1 John 2:3–11
Psalm 96
Luke 2:22–35

Wednesday

DECEMBER 30

Do not love the world or the things of the world.
—1 JOHN 2:15

How can we not love this beautiful world full of people
who are dear to us? In John's community, the *world* had
become a code word meaning "allurements that tempt us
away from Christ." The actor Sidney Poitier made a similar
point in his spiritual autobiography, *The Measure of a Man.*
Poitier puzzles how we've managed in this society to trade
the idea of our sacred humanity for the pitiful identity of
"consumers." Don't let anyone tell you you're a consumer!
You're heaven's child!

1 John 2:12–17
Psalm 96
Luke 2:36–40

⊰ 400 ⊱

He came to what was his own,
but his own people did not accept him.
But to those who did accept him he gave power to become children
of God. . . .

—JOHN 1:11–12

My brother was a Christmas baby, annually upstaged by a *bigger* birthday. So I feel a little sorry for Pope Sylvester I, whose fate it is to be perennially ignored on New Year's Eve. Sylvester baptized Emperor Constantine, who made Christianity legal. That action changed the world, although many argue that the change was not for the better. What if Christianity had remained a subversive movement, a crime punishable by death? Would the church be a more passionate, dedicated, if smaller assembly? How many of us would be Christians today?

1 John 2:18–21
Psalm 96
John 1:1–18